Minute Meditations for Couples

Bob and Emilie Barnes

HARVEST HOUSE PUBLISHERS
Eugene, Oregon 97402

Cover design by Terry Dugan Design, Minneapolis, Minnesota

MINUTE MEDITATIONS FOR COUPLES
Copyright © 2001 by Bob and Emilie Barnes
Published by Harvest House Publishers
Eugene, Oregon 97402

Library of Congress Catalog-in-Publication Data

Barnes, Bob, 1933-
    Minute meditations for couples / Bob and Emilie Barnes.
        p. cm.
    ISBN 0-7369-0548-0
        1. Married people—Prayer-books and devotions—English. I. Barnes,
    Emilie. II. Title.
BV4596.M3 B38 2001
242'.644—dc21   00-049853

Printed in the United States of America

01 02 03 04 05 / BC-BG / 10 9 8 7 6 5 4 3 2 1

From Emilie and Bob

Throughout Scripture we are encouraged to be united. Togetherness gives marriages a strength that is not seen in other social institutions. One aspect of the Christian church that gets attention from the world is the strength of its families. We've written this book so that you can grow together in your faith.

Minute Meditations for Couples gives both of you an opportunity to read, discuss, and pray together. If you aren't used to praying aloud, there are sample prayers you may use; however, if you are accustomed to praying together then use your own.

Another unique feature of this book is that you don't have to start at the beginning and go straight through. You can skip around to find the devotions that speak to you that day. At the top of each devotion there are three boxes. Put a check mark in one of the boxes each time you read that devotion. This way you can keep track of the readings you have shared previously.

At the end of each meditation, under "Reflection," we have included space to journal your thoughts. Jot down any items that were especially meaningful or that you would like to remember for future study.

We are all in a hurry doing our various things. These short devotions will encourage both of you to develop a habit of getting into God's Word together. Research has shown that if someone does an activity for 21 days in a row, a new habit will be formed.

This book was written while we were in Seattle taking care of Emilie's illness. May the meditations touch you as a couple, and may you be challenged to live a more godly life.

Thank You!

This book is dedicated to the many couples we have met at the Fred Hutchinson Cancer Research Center in Seattle, Washington. Each of you has been an inspiration to us. Your commitment and dedication to each other have been such an encouragement. We have often said that God only permits good people to have cancer. He knows the ones who can handle such a journey. Those couples at the "Hutch" for treatment have already been tested long before their arrival. It has been so touching to see how the caretakers have so lovingly attended to all the personal needs of their mates.

The courtesy, the love, the tenderness, the cuddling being freely exhibited show what tragedy does to bring couples closer together. To those of you who have been our support group we say, "Thank you!" Many of you we may never meet again, but for this brief time in our lives you have made the journey bearable.

A special dedication goes to the professional medical providers who took care of our every need. Your tender, loving support gave us a calm when many times we didn't know what to expect. You made the unknown bearable. Your bedside manners were such a comfort. For those in research spending hours, days, weeks, months, and years behind the microscope—we salute you. Without your dedication to curing this dreaded disease we would not have been able to undergo this radical treatment successfully.

We also want to say thank you to the staff that runs the Residence Inn by Marriott at Lake Union. Each of you greeted our days with a warm smile and a mention that you were praying for us. Each of our needs was met, and often you went beyond the call of duty. You truly care for those who stay in your hotel.

Let People Touch Your Star

I can do all things through Christ who strengthens me.
—PHILIPPIANS 4:13

Scripture Reading: Philippians 4:10-20

The burning of a little straw may hide the stars of the sky, but the stars are there, and will appear" (Carlyle). Have you ever considered that you are a star people can touch? Does your life light up the room when you enter? Do your children and grandchildren reflect the love you give them? Do the elderly say you make a difference in their lives? Yes, you can become a star in so many areas if you will only think in the larger terms of life.

We each have 24 hours a day, seven days a week. What are you going to do with your time? Most of the great conquests of life started as a little idea in someone's head—for example, Microsoft, Hewlett Packard, McDonald's, Coca-Cola, Weight Watchers, and Campus Crusade. It's what is done with that idea that counts.

Scripture says that without a vision a nation will perish—and so will we. As Christians, we either grow or we begin to slide backward. No one advances by accident; all achievements are reached by vision and hard work.

What are your deepest dreams—writing a song, starting a business, authoring a book, helping children, being a nurse, being a gourmet chef? Reach out today and plan how you are going to energize that thought into reality. Don't let the dream fall to the ground and die. Plant it, nurture it, and water it until God makes it grow. Daniel H. Burnham said, "Make no little plans, they have no magic to stir men's blood....Make big plans, aim high in hope and work."

Action

Dream a big dream today and share it with your spouse.

Prayer

Father God, we know You had a big plan when You created the world. We want to reach for the stars and go beyond. Amen.

Reflection

Twenty-Six Guards

Rejoice always, pray without ceasing.
—1 THESSALONIANS 5:16,17

Scripture Reading: 1 Thessalonians 5:12-22

One of the hardest disciplines is to remember to pray when we say we will. We have good intentions, but we forget. A missionary on furlough told this true story.

> While serving at a small field hospital in Africa, every two weeks I traveled by bicycle through the jungle to a nearby city for supplies. This was a journey of two days and required camping overnight at a halfway point. On one of these journeys, I arrived in the city and observed two men fighting, one of whom had been seriously injured. I treated him for his injuries and talked to him about the Lord Jesus Christ.
>
> Two weeks later, I repeated my journey. Upon arriving in the city, I was approached by the young man I had treated. He told me that he had known that I carried money and medicines. He said, "Some friends and I followed you into the jungle, knowing you would camp overnight. We planned to kill you and take your money and drugs. But

just as we were about to move into your camp, we saw that you were surrounded by 26 armed guards."

At this, I laughed and said that I was certainly all alone in that jungle campsite. The young man pressed the point, however, and said, "No, sir, I was not the only person to see the guards. My five friends also saw them, and we all counted them."

At this point in the sermon, one of the men in the congregation jumped to his feet and asked if the missionary could tell him the exact day this happened. The speaker told the congregation the date, then the man who interrupted said, "On the night of your incident in Africa, it was morning here and I was preparing to go play golf when I felt the urge to pray for you. In fact, the urging of the Lord was so strong that I called men in this church to meet with me in the sanctuary to pray for you. Would those men who met with me on that day stand up?" The men who had met together to pray that day stood up. There were 26![1]

This story is an incredible example of how the Spirit of God moves. If you ever experience prodding to pray, go along with it! God hears and answers prayers of the faithful.

Action

Join hands with your mate and pray for those in need.

Prayer

Father God, thanks for impressing upon us the need to continually be in prayer. Amen.

Reflection

Anyone Can Sing in the Sunshine

Beloved, do not think it strange concerning the fiery trial.
Rejoice to the extent you partake of Christ's suffering.
—1 PETER 4:12,13

Scripture Reading: 1 Peter 4:12-19

---

*R*ejoicing anytime is a delight to behold, but seeing someone who is able to rejoice when it is raining is particularly amazing. Sunshine rejoicing is a lot easier than raining rejoicing. When all's going well and we are bumping heaven, that's easy. It's much more impressive when the winds blow and rain begins to fall.

For most of our lives, we have lived a life with noon-day sunshine—not a cloud in the sky. For the last three-and-a-half years, however, we have had dark clouds hanging over our heads. Many times we were anticipating the medical profession telling us that there weren't any more treatments left for Emilie's type of lymphoma, but they didn't. When one new treatment failed there by grace was a new treatment available. During this rainy season of our lives we were able to rejoice in the Lord.

Once there was a godly woman who had suffered for several months with a lingering illness. One day while her pastor was visiting, she said, "I have such a lovely robin that sings outside my window. In the early morning, as I lie here, he serenades me." With a smile that radiated a deep joy within her weakened body, she added, "I love him because he sings in the rain."

This trait of the robin—singing when the storm has silenced other song birds—should be evidenced in a similar way by every child of God.

Throughout Scripture the writers have rejoiced even when the storm clouds come and it begins to violently rain. One of our sustaining verses of Scripture is found in John 11:4: "This sickness is not unto death, but for the glory of God, that the Son of God may be glorified through it."

Anyone can sing in the sunshine, but those who know Jesus as Savior can experience joy in the midst of a rainstorm. The psalmist in Psalm 61:8 writes, "So I will sing praise to Your name forever." Life teaches us that the sun doesn't always shine. Our joyfulness will be tested to see if we are more than sunshine believers. When the showers come, look upward and know that after every rain there will be rays of sunshine. "Weeping may endure for a night, but joy comes in the morning" (Psalm 30:5).

Action
When the rain begins to fall, rejoice.

Prayer
Father God, since Jesus Christ is Lord of heaven and earth, we can keep singing. Thank You for our mentors who teach us to rejoice when it rains. Amen.

Reflection

A Ship in the Night

*And you shall know the truth, and
the truth shall make you free.*
—JOHN 8:32

Scripture Reading: John 8:28-36

---

*I*sn't it difficult to change when you think you are right? We get so stubborn that we won't change our thoughts and opinions for anything. "Why should I? I'm right!" we say.

One foggy night the captain of a large ship saw another ship's lights approaching. This other ship was on a course that would mean a head-on crash. Quickly the captain signaled to the approaching ship, "Please change your course 10 degrees west." The reply came blinking back through the thick fog, "You change your course 10 degrees east."

Indignantly the captain pulled rank and shot a message back to the other ship, "I'm a sea captain with 35 years of experience. You change your course 10 degrees west!" Without hesitation the signal flashed back, "I'm a seaman fourth-class. You change your course 10 degrees east!"

Enraged, the captain realized that within minutes they would crash head-on, so he blazed his final warning: "I'm a 50,000-ton freighter. Change your course!" The simple message winked back, "I'm a lighthouse. You change..."[2]

You, too, may get so frustrated with your mate that you give out stern warnings that he or she had better change course. Because of past experiences, you and your spouse may not want to budge from your respective positions. Satan would like to destroy your marriage using the differences in the way you like to do things. We petition both of you today to be set free from stubbornness.

You must be willing to support one another (see Ephesians 5:21). With this attitude you are free to serve each other. Anything less than this allows selfishness and pride to enter your life, creating an unwillingness to change.

Alter your course rather than insisting on your own way.

Action

Think of one thing in your relationship that needs to be changed. Make the change.

Prayer

Father God, let us always remain flexible. We don't want to break apart when we move. Amen.

Reflection

Becoming Prominent

*Walk worthy of the calling with which you were called,
with all lowliness and gentleness.*
—EPHESIANS 4:1,2

Scripture Reading: Ephesians 4:1-16

It seems like everyone wants to become prominent—even if it's only for a short 15 minutes. We are often amazed at what people will do to accomplish this fame. Often their feats are difficult—and some are even death-defying and down-right dangerous.

One person may want to make a motorcycle jump across the Snake River in Idaho, another person chooses to swim across the English Channel, others will float in a hot air balloon across the continent or large body of water (some have even attempted to go around the world), some people get a thrill out of bungee jumping.

In God's plan, we are the happiest when we are content with what He has for us. It may be large or small, but finding where God wants us to serve—then doing it—is extremely fulfilling. Ask God to put you in that particular place of service for which you are suited and where prominence comes from the fruit you bear. You'll never lose your influence for Christ if you humbly seek to do His will.

Action

As a couple, discuss what motivates you to do what you do. Is it for you or is it for the glory of God?

Prayer

Father God, help us examine what motivates us to do what we do. Make it clear to us if we are off base. Thank You for this insight. Amen.

Reflection

One truth about God which I continue to discover anew is that he has more for us than we can imagine. His plans far exceed our plans, and his grace makes possible so much more than we can envision.

—NANCY PICKERING

Let Children Come

Let the little children come to Me...
—MARK 10:14

Scripture Reading: Mark 10:13-16

---

*J*esus had special compassion for children. Each time He was around them, He was touching, loving, and He even let them sit on His lap. He loved children and was aware that they needed special protection.

You've heard it said that a country will be judged by what it does to its children. It's sad how our country treats our little people. Each day we read countless stories of what some adults do to those children God has given to us for raising. All we have to do is talk to doctors and nurses in the emergency rooms of our local hospitals to discover they are very disturbed at the evidence of child abuse they see.

Quite often we see on TV pictures of starving children from third-world countries. And judgment will come hard someday to those of us who have stood by and known that countless millions of children have been aborted.

Today's society needs to reread the passages that Jesus gives regarding the young children. At one time He warned big people that anybody who caused these little ones to sin would be better off with a millstone around his neck and drowned in the sea (see Matthew 18:6).

A cheerful child is the reflection of the innocence of God. We have often said that we wanted our grandchildren to stay in the Garden of Eden as long as they could. Friend, as parents we need to protect our children from growing up too fast. We need to slow down and let them enjoy the very valuable youth portion of their lives. It would also go well with us if we, too, could carry on more childlike behavior. Stay young in heart and spirit. Observe what your children do for pleasure—a splash in the pool, a bowl of popcorn, skipping in the park, laughing at a funny situation—and join in. Even have an occasional pillow fight!

Action

Commit to love and protect your children.

Prayer

Father God, thank You for the precious gift of our children. Help us learn to love and protect them as You would want us to. Amen.

Reflection

Amazing Grace

For by grace you have been saved through faith.

—EPHESIANS 2:8

Scripture Reading: Ephesians 2:1-10

While celebrating our twenty-fifth wedding anniversary, we had the good fortune to cruise the Mexican waters on the "Love Boat." It was truly a wonderful experience. One of the highlights of our trip happened one Sunday evening as we were leaving the harbor of Acapulco. Bagpipers started playing the Christian anthem, "Amazing Grace." That five-minute concert was such a spiritual uplift that we have never forgotten it. It certainly added a positive insight to our salvation when we paused on the top deck of that large cruise ship and reflected that it is only by God's grace that we are saved.

In a small cemetery in a parish churchyard in Alney, England, stands a granite tombstone with the following inscription: "John Newton, Clerk, once an infidel and libertine, a servant of slavers in Africa, was, by the rich mercy of our Lord and Savior Jesus Christ, preserved, restored, pardoned, and appointed to preach the faith he had long labored to destroy."[3]

John Newton never ceased to marvel at the grace of God that had so dramatically transformed him from his early life as an African slave trader to a proclaimer of the glorious gospel of Christ. This was always the dominant theme of his preaching and writing. In 1779, Newton wrote these words: "Amazing grace! How sweet the sound that saved a wretch like me! I once was lost but now am found, was blind but now I see."

Even though we aren't slave traders, our sins are just as great. Without the grace of God we would all remain sinners doomed to eternal death, but with God's grace we can live eternally in heaven. We are saved through Jesus, not of ourselves and not of any of our works—salvation is a gift from God. Truly it is amazing grace!

Action
Give praises to God today for your salvation.

Prayer
Father God, thank You for Your free gift of grace. May we always appreciate Your love for us. Amen.

Reflection

Wash Your Own Windows

Why do you look at the speck in your brother's eye, but do not perceive the plank in your own eye?

—LUKE 6:41

Scripture Reading: Luke 6:37-42

While Emilie has been in cancer treatment, we have stayed at a condominium near the hospital. Since we are at the beach we have a lovely view of the west. We see some of the prettiest sunsets at evening tide, but recently the view seemed not as clear as it had been. The homes on the bluff across the way didn't seem as close or as impressive as in the beginning of our stay. I even considered going to my eye doctor to see if my vision had changed. One day as I was reflecting on this situation, Emilie with her wifelike wisdom asked, "Do you think we should wash the windows?" Guess what? When the windows were washed, I discovered I didn't need to see the eye doctor! The view was back to normal. I could again enjoy the scenery and the sunsets.

How often we overlook our own failures and sins while being critical of the situation. Are we looking through the smudges of our own lives and criticizing others? We must work on our own flaws before we try to help others with theirs.

Action

Take a plank from your eyes today.

Prayer

Father God, let us clean our eyes with a good eyewash so we can clearly see what we are looking at. Help us see what's wrong. Amen.

Reflection

Which One Is Adopted?

There is no partiality with God.
—ROMANS 2:11

Scripture Reading: Romans 2:1-11

Quite often in a family the children will ask Mom and Dad which child they love the most. For some reason they sense a partiality and would like to know for themselves who is the favorite. As parents, we have to be alert to this feeling and make sure there is no partiality. Each child is uniquely made by God. Here's a great illustration!

A Sunday school superintendent was registering two new boys in Sunday school. She asked their ages and birthdays so she could place them in the appropriate classes. The bolder of the two replied, "We're both seven. My birthday is April 8 and my brother's birthday is April 20." The superintendent replied, "But that's not possible, boys." The quieter brother spoke up. "No, it's true. One of us is adopted."

"Oh?" asked the superintendent, not convinced. "Which one?" The two brothers looked at each other and smiled. The bolder one said, "We asked Dad that same question awhile ago, but he just looked at us and said he loved us both equally, and he couldn't remember anymore which one of us was adopted."[4]

As adopted sons and daughters of God, we fully share in the inheritance of His only begotten Son, Jesus. If Jesus can love us equally, then we can surely give to our children with no partiality regarding blessings or privileges.

Action

Evaluate how we are doing raising our children with no partiality. Make changes where necessary.

Prayer

Father God, You are our example in raising our children. As believers, each of us has equal inheritances of blessings and privileges. Help us do the same for our children. Amen.

Reflection

Be Among Them

*Now both Jesus and His disciples were
invited to the wedding.*

—JOHN 2:2

Scripture Reading: John 2:1-11

Weddings are much more than beautiful gowns, crowds of people, and expensive decorations. It includes worship and giving thanks to God as well as the celebrating of the wonderful blessing God has given in a spouse.

Even though Jesus' ministry of three years was very serious and focused in nature, He still had time to enjoy Himself with His friends. All through the New Testament we read about relationships that meant a lot to Him. If we were in the midst of a wedding, I'm sure we would find Jesus celebrating with the bride and groom and conversing with others. He would most likely be laughing, talking, and enjoying Himself.

A wedding is also a time of commitment. It's an appropriate time to reflect on the unconditional love God has demonstrated. The couple commits to following the Lord in their home until "death do us part" (see Matthew 19:6). This commitment is more than just to the man and woman; it also includes commitment to our heavenly Father, who has committed Himself to the church (Ephesians 5:21-33). Two crucial elements to a wedding need to be present:

- The marriage should be established in the name of our Lord Jesus (Mark 10:9).

- Thanks must be given to God (Colossians 3:17). Weddings are a time of worship that celebrates each partner's commitment grounded in the love of God.

Our faith is very serious, but our religion is also one of relationships, conversations, celebrations, happiness, and laughter. We need to have a balanced life. If we haven't learned to enjoy the good times of life, we should begin now! Laughter and spending time with people are good for the soul.

Action
Give thanks for the happy times of life.

Prayer
Father God, may we not be so heavenly minded that we aren't any earthly good. Give us eyes and hearts that are opened to the joys of life. Amen.

Reflection

Nine Beautiful Words

The fruit of the Spirit is love, joy, peace, longsuffering,
kindness, goodness, faithfulness, gentleness, self-control.
—GALATIANS 5:22-23

Scripture Reading: Galatians 5:16-26

*I*n our Christian walks, we have discovered that many things are at work at any one given time. We have wanted to know how to take God's Word and live it out in our everyday actions. In essence, we wanted the fruit of the Spirit to be at work in our day-to-day life.

As we've read today's verse over the years, we tended to skim over each descriptive trait without truly seeking what the Scripture has to say about each one. But now, as we have looked at these all-powerful nine words individually and more closely, we realize that these nine words describe how we want to be known in our Christian walks. These words have become a symbol of grace as we live out our faith.

As Christians, if we could make these words the spiritual goals of our lives, we could have incredible influence on the world around us. Our churches would be overflowing with people as we lovingly attend to the needs of the lost. And the whole world would be lifted up by the sweet fragrance of forgiveness and acceptance!

Study and meditate on the fruit of the Spirit. As you become aware of the power of each word and grasp why Paul used these particular terms to illustrate the goodness of the gospel, may the Holy Spirit empower you to reflect these traits in your daily lives:

- Love
  - Joy
    - Peace
      - Longsuffering
        - Kindness
          - Goodness
            - Faithfulness
              - Gentleness
                - Self-Control

Action

Take one of these words and implement it in your life today.

Prayer

Father God, may we learn how to live out the fruit of the Spirit in a meaningful way that has a healing effect on a hurting world. Amen.

Reflection

Say No to Rage

Let all bitterness, wrath, anger, clamor, and evil speaking be
put away from you, with all malice.
—EPHESIANS 4:31

Scripture Reading: Ephesians 4:25-32

Two shoppers in a Connecticut supermarket get in a fistfight over who should be first in a newly opened checkout lane. A high-school baseball coach in Florida breaks an umpire's jaw after arguing over a disputed call. At a hockey game two fathers get in a fight over rough play; one father dies due to injuries incurred in the fight. An airplane returns to the airport after a passenger throws a can of beer at a flight attendant and bites a pilot who tries to assist the attendant.

The media reports incidents of road rage, biker rage, surfer rage, airplane rage, grocery store rage, and rage in professional sports. Leading health experts state that our nation is in the middle of an anger epidemic that in its mildest forms is unsettling and at its worst, deadly. They blame an increasing sense of self-importance and the widespread selfish belief that "our" way is better.

A young man who had been insulted by a friend was very upset. "I'm going at once to demand an apology," he insisted. "My dear boy," cautioned a wise man, "take a word of advice from one who loves peace. An insult is like mud; it will brush off much better when it dries. Wait until you and he cool off, and the thing will be easily solved. If you go now, it will only be a quarrel." The young man listened to that wise counsel, and the next day the person who had insulted him came to ask for his forgiveness.

How does this relate to us? When we are offended allow reaction time. Our first reaction is usually not the best reaction. Remember that time and God are on our side.

Action

When things don't go right for you today, remember that mud brushes off better when it is dry.

Prayer

Father God, we pray that we might use this example within our own relationship. Let no unwholesome words come out of our mouths. Help us give each other time to reflect and evaluate instead of reacting on the spot. Amen.

Reflection

Living a Higher Purpose

Seek those things which are above, where Christ is, sitting at the right hand of God.
—COLOSSIANS 3:1

Scripture Reading: Colossians 3:1-4

So, you've made a few million dollars in your life. You own a mansion in Connecticut, a fleet of Jaguars, a Lear jet, and a house on St. Barts Island in the French West Indies. So what's left? Well, a yacht would be nice—but not any yacht. Not the 100-foot boats your friends own. No, you deserve something more. Something grander. Something closer to 200 feet in the $35 million range. Yes, that would do nicely.

We have often heard the adage, "He who dies with the most toys wins." However, I've never heard of a man on his deathbed who wished he had owned a bigger toy. His last, fleeting moments usually are filled with thoughts of how he could have loved his family more.

The sad fact of life is that many of us live the philosophy that who has the most possessions wins. We all like to be around big toys, and we like to play with them. But to spend our whole lives for such things seems a lot like having a large diamond and playing marbles in the mud with it.

In order for us to have meaning to life, we must have a higher purpose, and Jesus shows us the way. He did not come to earth to play with toys or to see how much pleasure He could enjoy. He came to serve and to give us salvation. God knows how our earthly nature tries to enslave us. In Matthew 6:33, He challenges us to "seek first the kingdom of God and His righteousness." In Colossians 3:2, He says, "Set your mind on things above." Don't look to the world for direction. Look to God.

Action

Look upward today and see what God has for your life.

Prayer

Father God, give us a proper understanding of why we are here. May we enjoy the abundances of life by first seeking Your kingdom. Amen.

Reflection

The Big "C"

Then Isaac...took Rebekah and she
became his wife, and he loved her.
—GENESIS 24:67

Scripture Reading: Genesis 24:61-67

---

oday we often hear of a dissatisfied mate who wants to file for divorce uttering these words, "The chemistry is gone." In reading Scripture he or she has not grasped the true "C" of the Bible. It isn't chemistry, but it is commitment. Couples today are confused about marriage. For some reason we have abandoned the real concept of unity and bought into the false belief that marriage is warm, fuzzy, and has bells and whistles that shoot into the air when the lights go dark. This is Hollywood's version.

We love to hear stories from couples who have been married for a long period of time. All have had rocky roads along the way, but they share a common characteristic—they have endured. They express their joy by saying, "I'm so glad we stuck it out. Now we are receiving God's blessing for being obedient. "Old-fashioned, life-time commitments. True love endures in spite of difficulties. Paul says, "Love never fails" (1 Corinthians 13:8).

Create a deep desire in your heart and soul to look after the welfare of your mate. Let it grow and become more enduring the older you become.

Action

Show your spouse that you are committed to your marriage.

Prayer

Father God, give us the inspiration to have the right "C" in our marriage. Amen.

Reflection

A Built-In Security System

*The LORD shall preserve your going out and your coming in
from this time forth, and even forevermore.*

—PSALM 121:8

Scripture Reading: Psalm 121

During the last three years of battling cancer, we have had times when we had to have reassurances from our many friends that God had not forgotten us. Sometimes it seemed like our prayers weren't being answered. Yes, our faith was strong and we still believed with all our hearts, but we needed added Scriptures and prayers for support.

A very energetic and self-confident older woman told her pastor, "I don't need Christ in the daytime while I'm awake. I can take care of myself. But I do pray at night when I'm asleep. In fact, I've said bedtime prayers since I was a child."

We know a lot of people who seem more than capable of taking care of themselves during the light period of day, but they aren't quite as confident when the sun sets. During this season of illness, we can tell you that we have experienced prayer needs 24 hours a day, 7 days a week,

52 weeks a year. It is so reassuring to know that the Lord preserves us while we go out and when we come in. God always protects us. He is a great security system.

Action

Step out today and trust God for the little things of life.

Prayer

Father God, how awesome You are to know and care about all our needs. We thank You for watching out for us. Amen.

Reflection

Cancer is so limited...

It cannot cripple Love
It cannot shatter Hope
It cannot corrode Faith
It cannot destroy Peace
It cannot kill Friendship
It cannot suppress Memories
It cannot silence Courage
It cannot invade the Soul
It cannot steal eternal Life
It cannot conquer the Spirit

—AUTHOR UNKNOWN

Establishing Stable Boundaries

A merry heart makes a cheerful countenance, but by sorrow of the heart the spirit is broken.
—PROVERBS 15:13

Scripture Reading: Proverbs 3:11,12; 13:24; 15:13

Raising children is an awesome task that seems overwhelming at times. How to discipline is one of the most difficult aspects of this area. The natural tendency is to throw in the towel and give up. How do we set and maintain stable boundaries?

Proverbs 13:24 tells us that if we truly love our children, we will discipline them diligently. This does not mean we are to be abusive, unfair, or degrading. The discipline comes from *love* not hate. It upholds the child's worth and is fair and fitting for the infraction. Also, the child must understand the discipline he is to receive. Spend plenty of time discussing with the child what was improper. Make sure he understands what the infraction was.

One of the main purposes of discipline is to let the children know they are responsible for their actions and accountable for their behaviors. In our home, we applied the discipline when warranted, then after a 15 to 30 minute break for reflection, the situations usually ended in prayer, along with warm hugs and assuring words.

Action

As a couple be sure to have a clear direction regarding the goal of your children's discipline. It's very important that you are clear and in agreement.

Prayer

Father God, give us wisdom to know what kind of discipline will be effective for each child. Amen.

Reflection

*To love your child
unconditionally is to
determine that no
matter what, you will
always seek his highest
good, not your own.*

—JAN SILVIOUS

Not a River of Disappointment

Jesus said to him, "I am the way, the truth, and the life.
No one comes to the Father except through Me."
—JOHN 14:6

Scripture Reading: John 14:6-11

With every edition of the monthly magazines that appear on the stands at our supermarkets, we see more featured articles on other religions of the world than those on Christian heritage. While staying in Seattle, we have observed the diversity of worship. It would be very easy to be fooled by those who teach a way to God other than through our Lord, Jesus Christ.

Sir Alexander Mackenzie is a Canadian hero. He was an early fur trader and explorer who accomplished marvelous feats when he led an expedition across Canada to the Pacific Ocean. His journey was completed in 1793, eleven years before Lewis and Clark began their famous expedition to the west. Mackenzie's earlier attempt in 1789, however, had been a major disappointment. His explorers had set out in an effort to find a water route to the Pacific. The valiant group followed a mighty river, now named the Mackenzie. Unfortunately, it didn't empty into the Pacific as hoped but into the Arctic Ocean. In his diary Mackenzie called it the "River of Disappointment."

As we journey through life looking for the straight and narrow path to God, we don't want to end our journey and declare it "a river of disappointment."

In our reading for today Jesus assuredly pronounces, "I am the way, the truth, and the life. No one comes to the Father except through Me."

Action

Take out your road map—the Bible. Are you on the right course?

Prayer

Father God, thank You for protecting us and helping us stay on the right course so our journey will not be a disappointment. Amen.

Reflection

Live by Faith

But that no one is justified by the law in the sight of God is evident, for "the just shall live by faith."

—GALATIANS 3:11

Scripture Reading: Galatians 3:10–4:11

As human beings we want to start our Christian walk as giants. We don't want to recognize that we must start at the bottom or in our current state. Our faith starts as a string, then develops into a cord, then a rope, then a larger rope, and finally a cable. In our world of comparisons we want to start right away as a cable because that's what we see around us. But, spiritual growth results from trusting in God the Father, God the Son, and God the Holy Spirit with more of our lives each day. In today's verse we see that the righteous person lives by faith. That faith must have an object and, for the Christian, that object is Jesus Christ. He came to atone for our sins; through Him we have forgiveness of our sins and a direct line to God the Father.

A life of faith will enable you to trust God increasingly with every detail of your life together, and decide each day to follow Jesus. The fruits and blessings of today are based upon the decisions you made yesterday.

Action

Decide to follow Jesus today. What act will you do?

Prayer

Father God, help us stay focused on what's important. Amen.

Reflection

～～～～～～～～～～

The more you trust God, the more you will come to know His character and to stare in amazement at what He has done in your life and to wait in anticipation for what He's going to do next. Thank you Lord for helping me to trust you.

—GLENN BAXLEY, EMILIE BARNES

～～～～～～～～～～

Encourage Your Pastor

Remember those who rule over you, who have spoken the word of God to you.
—HEBREWS 13:7

Scripture Reading: Hebrews 13:7-17

A pastor friend of ours recalls a large Promise Keepers gathering in Los Angeles where the master of ceremonies requested that all pastors in the crowd come onto the football field. As thousands of faithful pastors came forward, the remaining 60,000 men in the stadium stood up and started to clap, shout, and whistle. The roar became deafening. The applause lasted for at least ten minutes. Recognition for the pastors' faithfulness in ministry was long overdue. As the emcee finished giving honor to these servants of God, the audience again gave another standing ovation. Our friend said tears came down his cheeks as he heard such approval from those in attendance.

Have you taken the time to encourage your pastors for their role in feeding the flock of God and overseeing their spiritual welfare? We often take for granted that week after week our ministers will study and prepare a sermon that will reach us with God's truth. Often they feel unappreciated. Though they aren't looking for praise, they do need the encouragement of those who are helped by their ministries.

Action

Encourage your pastor today.

Prayer

Father God, thank You for giving us a wonderful pastor who encourages our walk with You. Please bless his life and ministry. Amen.

Reflection

~~~~~~~

*Enrich someone's life
today with a warm word
of praise. Both of you
will be better for it.*

—AUTHOR UNKNOWN

~~~~~~~

I Feel So Inadequate

"Do not be afraid of their faces, for I am with you to deliver you," says the LORD.

—JEREMIAH 1:8

Scripture Reading: Jeremiah 1:1-10

Have you ever been asked to make a presentation in front of a group? One of the most terrifying experiences I had while in high school was when my teacher announced that we had to give an oral book report. I felt so inadequate standing there in front of my classmates. I was afraid that I wouldn't be good enough.

As a young man, Jeremiah was called by God to carry a message of judgment to the people of Judah. At first he refused because of his inexperience and youth; however, the Lord assured Jeremiah that He would supply the power to do the task. David Livingstone, the great missionary and explorer, had spoken at a communion service in a Scottish chapel. The people asked him to stay overnight and preach the next morning. He agreed to do so if his friends would spend the night praying. But when Livingstone awoke, he was overwhelmed by such a great sense of inadequacy

43

that he left town. When his friends learned that he had fled, they caught up with him and brought him back. Then, trusting God's faithfulness and enablement, he preached with power, and many were converted to Christ.

When you are facing a monumental challenge, remember the promise that God gave Jeremiah in today's verse. Friends, be assured that God will provide when you feel inadequate.

Action

Rejoice in your weaknesses and trust in God's power.

Prayer

Father God, we know from experience that we are the strongest when we feel the weakest. The Holy Spirit comes in and gives us just the right words to think and say. Thanks for showing us that even when we are weak we can endure with Your power. Amen.

Reflection

Be Known for Love

And now abide faith, hope, love, these three;
but the greatest of these is love.

—1 CORINTHIANS 13:13

Scripture Reading: 1 Corinthians 13:1-13

All of us spend a good part of our lives earnestly searching for the most rewarding feeling of all—love. As tiny babies, we look to those around us to give us love. Later on, we read books and magazines, attend seminars and workshops, and have long conversations with others to improve our understanding of this concept. But despite our best efforts, we still have a hard time defining *love*. So what is this sought-after feeling? According to Scripture, it's much more than just a fleeting emotion. Love is a decision that we consciously make, and it's shown in how we treat other people. When we love them, we choose to do what is best for them.

The ultimate example of this kind of love is found in the primary love God has for us: "For God so loved the world that He gave His only begotten Son" (John 3:16). Now that's love! In spite of our not always choosing to do things His way, God sent His only Son so that we might be forgiven and delight in His everlasting caring. When we are able to capture the magnitude of His love for us, we gain an immense understanding of what living is all about. We gradually discover that He has placed in us a capacity to love others far beyond what we could ever imagine. Through this we can begin to love God, ourselves, and others.

Action

Love someone unconditionally today.

Prayer

Father God, please continue to remind us that we need to show Your love to someone else. Let people see You through my life. Amen.

Reflection

Chasing a Dark Maze

But as many as received Him, to them He gave the right to become children of God.

—JOHN 1:12

Scripture Reading: John 1:1-14

Most religions of the world reflect humanity's efforts to know God and become acceptable to Him. By contrast, Christianity begins with the Creator of heaven and earth reaching down to us. Someone once said that the difference between religion and Christianity is that religion is our attempt to reach up to God, whereas Christianity is a relationship between us and Jesus Christ.

We are able to go directly to God because of what Jesus did on the cross for our sins. Our part is to confess that we are sinners, to turn away from all efforts to earn our salvation, and to trust Him as our Savior.

Salvation is not something we achieve or work for. It is something we receive as a free gift!

Action

If you haven't accepted Christ as your personal Savior, do so now.

Prayer

> Father God, I no longer want to go through life's maze of earning my way to Your favor. I accept Your free gift of salvation. I choose to make Jesus my Lord and acknowledge His sacrifice for my sins. God, thank You for giving me the true light of the living God—You. Amen.

Reflection

〜〜〜〜〜〜〜

Experience the perfect peace of God in your life by realizing anew that it is only obtained through the presence of Christ in our lives—He is peace.

—KENNETH W. OSBECK

〜〜〜〜〜〜〜

Who Cares?

*Look on my right hand and see, for there is no one
who acknowledges me; refuge has failed me;
no one cares for my soul.*

—PSALM 142:4

Scripture Reading: Psalm 142:1-7

*W*ith increasing teenage and college-age suicides we hear the cry, "No one cares for me! No one!" A white collar worker in a towering office building goes bankrupt. Who cares? A punch press operator in a sprawling factory dies in a rush-hour traffic accident. Who cares? A teenager is shot by a drive-by shooter and dies. Who cares?

We live in an age when depersonalization, estrangement, isolation, and loneliness characterize our society. We tend to go right along with the crowd by pretending we're content. But inside, many of us feel alone, desperately alone. We seek acceptance in strange ways: We dye our hair funny colors, tattoo our bodies, join gangs, puncture our bodies, and add rings. Belonging to country clubs, playing bridge, joining service organizations, becoming church members, and participating in activist groups can be a way to acceptance. Even with all this "joining," many people still feel unloved.

Beneath our facade of coolness, we struggle with disconcerting doubts, lingering fears, and paralyzing anxieties. Silently we cry out for someone who will listen, who will care, and who will understand. Many of us agree with the psalmist who wrote today's verse. "Is there anyone who cares?" Jesus says in Mark 8:36, "What will it profit a man if he gains the whole world, and loses his own soul?" Here is someone who cares because He recognizes the worth of one single soul. *Jesus cares!* He is also the one who states, "Are not two sparrows sold for a copper coin? And not one of them falls to the ground apart from your Father's will. But the very hairs of your head are all numbered. Do not fear, therefore; you are of more value than many sparrows" (Matthew 10:29-31).

To accept Jesus' love is to find real peace and real assurance in this age of insecurity. He "will never leave you nor forsake you" (Hebrews 13:5).

Action

Share with someone today that you care about them. Tell them about Jesus' love!

Prayer

Father God, we thank You for caring for us. Your love has given us hope for today. May we pass that hope on to someone else today. Amen.

Reflection

Only Eighteen Inches

I have set the LORD always before me; because He is at my right hand I shall not be moved.

—PSALM 16:8

Scripture Reading: Psalm 16:7-10

Did you know that at any moment of your life, you're only 18 inches away from the hope you need? It's absolutely true. But it is also true that those 18 inches may be the longest distance you'll ever travel. Eighteen inches. That's the approximate distance from the top of your head to your heart. That's the critical distance you have to travel in order to live with an enduring, unquenchable hope.

You see, you can't live in your head only and live in hope. Enduring hope has to reside in your heart—the seat of all your emotions, your will, your connection with meaning. Hope comes when you invite the God who made you, the Christ who redeemed you, the Spirit who surrounds you—the triune God—to travel the same 18-inch journey from your head to your heart.

"How do you make the trip?" You have to take a leap of faith, which is not easy. You have to weigh the evidence—the testimony of the Bible; the life experiences of other people; and the still, small voice in your heart that keeps encouraging you to accept Jesus as your Savior. You've simply got to take a deep breath and make that "small," bottomless jump. Once you've done it, your hope for your life increases dramatically.[5]

Action

Make the journey if you haven't already. If you have—rejoice!

Prayer

Father God, thank You for letting us draw near to You. Truly our hope is in You! Amen.

Reflection

～～～～～～～～～

In Christ, there is freedom from bondage. Believers are no longer slaves; they are free—not through their own merit but through God's redeeming grace.

—RHONDA H. KELLEY

～～～～～～～～～

Any Place Is the Right Place

And they went out and preached everywhere.
—MARK 16:20

Scripture Reading: Mark 16:14-20

As Christians we are certainly diversified in what style we use in witnessing about our Savior, Jesus Christ. We see some people dragging a wooden cross around the world, some preaching on street corners, some dressing like Jesus and passing out Christian literature, some preaching from pulpits, some witnessing by living a godly lifestyle. Whatever our bent, we are to share our love for Jesus with others.

One of the most unusual approaches happened in the seventh game of the 1962 World Series. The San Francisco Giants had a man on second base, which put him near New York Yankee second baseman, Bobby Richardson. When the Yanks decided to change pitchers, Bobby, who was a Christian, saw a unique opportunity. While the new pitcher was warming up, he walked over to the man on second and asked him if he knew Jesus as his Savior. When the runner reached the dugout later, he asked teammate Felipe Alou, who also was a Christian, what was going on: "Even in the seventh game of the World Series," he said to Felipe, "you people are still talking about Jesus."

Be creative in your style. Not everyone will want to hear the "good news" of the gospel, but those who do will shout with joy when they discover they can talk to someone who cares about them.

Action

Witness today in a very unusual way or place.

Prayer

Father God, give us the opportunity today to share with someone how Your Son gave His life to set us free. Amen.

Reflection

~~~~~~~~~~

*Lord, You are the beginning,
the end, and the very essence
of love in me. Open my eyes
to see as You see, and love
others through me.*

—SANDY SMITH

~~~~~~~~~~

When It's Hard to Love

Hatred stirs up strife, but love covers all sins.
—PROVERBS 10:12

Scripture Reading: Proverbs 10:1-12

As we read the morning newspaper or view the evening news, we are saddened to read and hear of the tragic murder of children by restless, irresponsible people who decide the kids should be killed. We seem to live in a hate-generated society that doesn't value another person's life. We often ask, "How do parents live through the murder of an innocent child?" Only through God's love can a heart of hate be changed to a heart of love.

In January 1981, Colombian rebels kidnapped Chet Bitterman, held him for 48 days, shot him, and left his body in a hijacked bus. Imagine how his parents and loved ones must have felt at the senseless death of this young man. But in April 1982, as a demonstration of international goodwill, the churches and civic groups of Bitterman's native area, Lancaster County, Pennsylvania, gave an ambulance to the state of Meta in Colombia, where the young Wycliffe linguist was killed.

Bitterman's parents traveled to Colombia for the presentation of the ambulance. At the ceremony his mother shared, "We are able to do this because God has taken the hatred from our hearts."

Action

Turn any hatred you might have into love.

Prayer

Father God, thank You for protecting us from any hate-producing events in our lives. Help us support those who have hearts of love. Amen.

Reflection

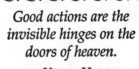

*Good actions are the
invisible hinges on the
doors of heaven.*

—Victor Hugo

Life That Lasts Forever

He who believes in Me has everlasting life.
—JOHN 6:47

Scripture Reading: John 6:35-51

By our nature, we ask two basic questions regarding our tenure on life:

1. How long will I live?

2. When will the earth end?

With the increased gambling and lottery playing in our states, the populous is being led down a dead-end street that could threaten their present—and future—lives.

While leading a weekly Bible study a few years ago, we had a member who shared with us that he became a Christian for "fire" insurance. He didn't want to risk his future by not believing in Jesus. Unfortunately his life also reflected that kind of commitment. He was neither cold nor hot, and his life bore no fruit. He was just trying to get by for his future destination.

You don't have to play the guessing game on how you will live each day as an authentic Christian. Jesus promises in today's verse that once your life is safely in His hands you have everlasting life with your heavenly Father. Then the issues of how long your earthly life will last and how long the world will go on are less important.

Jesus' promise is in the present tense—not something far away in the future. It means that believers have everlasting life *now*.

In reality, everyone will have eternal life. You must decide where—either with Jesus in heaven or experiencing the torments of hell.

Action

Decide today with whom you will live eternally.

Prayer

Father God, thank You for the opportunity to live eternally with You. May we receive and live out that gift. Amen.

Reflection

The Ultimate Helper

And I will pray the Father, and He will give you another
Helper, that He may abide with you forever.
—JOHN 14:16

Scripture Reading: John 14:16-26

Holy Spirit, faithful Guide,
Ever near the Christian's side,
Gently lead us by the hand
Pilgrims in a desert land.
—MARCUS WELLS, 1858

A gentleman was struggling to get to Grand Central Station in New York City during extreme weather conditions. The wind blew fiercely and the rain beat down on him as he carried his two heavy suitcases toward the train station. He was only able to go short distances at a time because his strength would not hold up for very long. At several points he was ready to give up. At his last pause, a man appeared at his side and picked up the suitcases. He said, "You look as if you could use some help, and I'm going in the same direction."

When they reached the terminal and were inside, away from the weather, this weary traveler, the renowned doctor Booker T. Washington, asked the man, "Please, sir, what is your name?" The man replied, "The name, my friend, is Roosevelt. Teddy Roosevelt."

We, too, don't have to stand alone during our time of need. It is not our battle alone. God gave us the Holy Spirit to come alongside of us to help. The Holy Spirit will strengthen us during those times when we don't think we can go one more step.

Action

Reach out today and call on the Holy Spirit to be your comforter. He will come alongside and ease the load.

Prayer

Father God, even though we feel we can handle our own situations, let us humbly bow and call upon You to help us with our burdens. Amen.

Reflection

Redeeming Time

*Walk in wisdom toward those who are
outside, redeeming the time.*
—COLOSSIANS 4:5

Scripture Reading: Colossians 4:1-6

---

*G*od delights in bringing order from confusion
and turning weaknesses into strengths. He
redeems our time as well as our toils.

In Scripture the concept of organization deals far more
with our relationships than with possessions or circumstances. When life is in order, we have smoother commu-
nication, more effective problem solving, efficient task
management, better interpersonal relationships, and
clearer understanding of what needs to be done.

God wants us to be organized so that our lives will be
free of chaos and stress, which gives us the maximum freedom for achieving His goals for our lives.

Each of us must come to grips with order in our own
way. Some basic components are:

- Start with yourself. Find out what causes confusion in your life. Establish your own plan on
  what changes must be made.

- Keep it simple. Don't make your plans too
  complicated.

- Have designated places for everything. Avoid piling up papers, toys, clothes, and so on.

- Store like items together. Designate certain places for specific groups: bills, invoices, coffee/tea items, gardening tools, laundry, and so on.

- Get rid of items you don't use. If you haven't used the item in the last year, give it away, throw it away, or have a garage sale.

- Invest in proper tools. Use bins, hooks, racks, containers, lazy Susans to maintain order.

- Keep master lists. Keep an inventory of where things are stored in binders, file cards, a computer, or journals.

- Use labels and signs. Label everything—specific items, drawers, and bins.

Action

Start today in reducing confusion and stress in your life.

Prayer

Father God, help us redeem our time by eliminating those things that rob us of time spent with You. Amen.

Reflection

Seek Safety in Surrender

Follow Me.
—LUKE 9:59

Scripture Reading: Luke 9:57-62

---

*I*n our hearts we want to follow Jesus, but we often give reasons why we don't: My job takes up so much time; my parents are in a nursing home; I'm getting a promotion. So many excuses. Sometimes we try to stay connected to God and still maintain control of what we want out of life.

Imagine you're in an apartment and outside the window is a large power line that carries a heavy current of electricity. It is carefully insulated at every pole and is high off the ground. If you could lean out far enough to grasp the wire, death would be as swift as a lightning strike. Yet the birds in the area suffer no such harm when they perch on the wire. They sit there in safety and contentment.

The secret of this marvel is that when the birds contact the wire, they touch nothing else. Because the birds rest only on the wire, they are protected and unharmed. If you reach out and touch the wire, you will still have your body in contact with the building—you would be grounded. The electrical current would turn your body into a channel through which the electricity would flow in fatal power.

How does this principle relate to our spiritual walk? We need to have both of our hands connected to our heavenly Father. We need to consecrate our lives to Him and not be grounded to the world. For example, we shouldn't put ourselves in danger by running and maintaining relations with the wrong crowd.

Action

Make sure that your hands are hanging on to God's.

Prayer

Father God, we pray that we will put worldly desires away from us. Let Your power flow through us in a mighty way. Amen.

Reflection

Take Time to Rest

Come to Me, all you who labor and are
heavy laden, and I will give you rest.
—MATTHEW 11:28

Scripture Reading: Matthew 11:25-30

---

*I*f you've ever gone to the Grand Canyon in Arizona, you have seen those burden-bearing donkeys that carry goods, people, and materials down to the canyon floor. They seem so small yet they carry such heavy loads that it's easy to feel sorry for these animals. As you look at their swaybacks, it doesn't seem like they can continue one more step. It's sort of like the pickup truck that's overloaded with sand and gravel. You know the springs are going to break.

Jesus saw people that way—burdened and stressed, weighed down by the legalism and legalistic demands the Pharisees had placed on them. No matter where they turned, some politician was telling them what to do or what not to do. Matthew 23:4 states: "For they bind heavy burdens, hard to bear, and lay them on men's shoulders; but they themselves will not move them with one of their fingers."

We don't need religion that becomes an unbearable burden. We need rest from the terrible burden that sin and hopelessness create. That's why Jesus came. He came to give us rest. By lifting the weight of sin from our shoulders, God opened the way for full and free living as He originally intended for us. To walk in obedience is never a burden—it's freedom.

It is also physically healthy to rest from the stresses of life. In order to live a long life, we must reduce the pressures in our lives. Prioritizing will help us cast off the hurry of today's technological age. Never in the history of mankind have we as people been under more pressure to perform. We are molded into thinking that we must have a perfect marriage, a perfect family, a perfect career, a perfect home. Because of this pressure, we will break if we don't relax. Jesus says to come unto Him and He will give us rest.

Action

Make sure you take time to rest.

Prayer

Father God, we don't know what life would be like if You weren't alongside us to ease our burden. You have given us great relief. Thank You. Amen.

Reflection

Clothe Yourselves with Humility

All of you be submissive to one another, and be clothed with humility, for "God resists the proud, but gives grace to the humble."

—1 PETER 5:5

Scripture Reading: 1 Peter 5:5-11

Wherever we are we hear trash talk. In athletics, sitcoms, movies, literature, schools, art, music, and business we see evidence of people who want to put down people in order to build themselves up. A true key to having successful relationships is humility. But humility is a difficult characteristic because once you think of yourself as humble—you're not!

Business literature talks about climbing the corporate ladder, upward mobility, self-assertion, and winning through intimidation. The focus is always on moving up. God's focus is different. The way up with God is always being humble in spirit. When Peter tells us to be clothed with humility, it is an exhortation not just a suggestion. The moment we allow pride to raise its ugly head in our hearts, the resistance of God begins. God opposes the proud. When you are clothed with humility, God ends His resistance against you. When we are humble, He promises to exalt us at the proper time.

Action

In what areas do you struggle with pride? What can you do to change your focus?

Prayer

Father God, please make us aware of any false pride in our lives. May the humility that comes from truly knowing You characterize all that we say or do. Amen.

Reflection

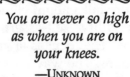

You are never so high as when you are on your knees.

—Unknown

Be Joyful

These things I have spoken to you, that My joy may remain in you, and that your joy may be full.
—JOHN 15:11

Scripture Reading: John 15:11-17

Many times we expect the fruit of joy to bring us unlimited happiness and fun times. Yet when we read the Scriptures, we are encouraged to reflect on what it really means to have a joyful heart. Happiness and fun are good in themselves, but they come and go. Joy, however, is felt beyond our circumstances. Joy exists even when times are difficult because it is an attitude we have toward life's experiences. It is a treasure of the heart, the comfort of knowing God's intimate presence.

As we view the events of our lives, we can choose to be resentful toward God for letting certain things happen to us or we can choose an attitude of gratitude and a commitment to joy. Joy is our best choice. We have joy when we are serving God and doing what He wants for our lives. We have joy when we learn to take circumstances and the ups and downs of life in stride and use all situations to bring glory to Jesus. We lighten our load in life and draw others to us by having a joyful heart. When we have joy in the Lord, we begin to see life from God's point of view. We will realize that things have never looked so beautiful, so peaceful, so amazing. The joy of the Lord is our strength.

Action

Find joy in your most difficult situation.

Prayer

Father God, we want to be known as joyful people—people who reflect the positive side of life. Amen.

Reflection

❦❦❦❦❦❦❦

The true test of walking in the Spirit will not be the way we act but the way we react to the daily frustrations of life.

—BEVERLY LaHAYE

❦❦❦❦❦❦❦

It's Not Too Late

Delight yourself also in the LORD, and
He shall give you the desires of your heart.
—PSALM 37:4

Scripture Reading: Psalm 37:1-11

Many of you who are reading this today are becoming discouraged with life or beginning to feel a sense of emptiness. Maybe work isn't going so well (you were recently passed over for a promotion), the children don't seem to appreciate what you do for them, or your marriage doesn't have the romance it once had. The purpose of life seems a little fuzzy. What can you do?

Start delighting in the Lord! As you take your eyes off yourself and focus on God and His eternal values by praying, reading the Bible, becoming active in a small support group, and actively trying to do His will, your perspective will change. As your desires begin to coincide with God's, He'll give you the desires of your heart. Only by putting God first will you find happiness and meaning.

Action

Be willing to make some drastic changes in your life. Focus on what God desires for you.

Prayer
　　Father God, teach us how to delight in Your ways. May
　　Your ways become our ways. Amen.

Reflection

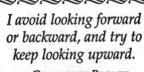

*I avoid looking forward
or backward, and try to
keep looking upward.*

—CHARLOTTE BRONTE

The Winning Team

Do you not know that those who run in a race all run, but one receives the prize? Run in such a way that you may obtain it.
—1 CORINTHIANS 9:24

Scripture Reading: 1 Corinthians 9:24-27

Sports on TV are so easily found while surfing the channels that we have become knowledgeable about a multitude of different activities. From our armchairs, we sometimes think we could accomplish what we watch others do. But the 63 for Tiger Woods or the 27 points for Kobe Bryant, or the 3 home runs in one game by Mark McGwire are phenomenal feats that few can duplicate. One of our favorite quotations is: The quality of a person's life is in direct proportion to his commitment to excellence.

Paul is a favorite biblical character because he was an outstanding competitor and someone who would never quit. What made his career so amazing was that while he was an ardent, follow-the-law Pharisee he had made it his job to rid the world of Christians. But on his way to Damascus to bring back some of the captured Christians for trial, Paul had a marvelous encounter with God. Paul is the person who penned our reading today in 1 Corinthians. He encourages us to run the race to win. In order for us to win the contest, we must deny ourselves many things that would keep us from doing our best. An athlete goes to all this trouble to win a blue ribbon or a gold medal, but we do it for a heavenly reward that never disappears.

Paul knows what it takes to be a champion. He says that in a race, everyone runs but only one person wins first prize—so run your race to win. We are all striving to be the people God created us to be and to share God's message of love. Paul says, "If you're going to take the challenge, win." He also says that we will pay a price to be a winner. A present-day saying is, "No pain—no gain." There is no easy way to success. We have to work hard.

Action

Go out and discipline your life for that heavenly reward.

Prayer

Father God, give us the excitement needed to run the race to win. We don't want to be just spectators. We want to be real participants who are willing to pay the price for being servants to those in need. Amen.

Reflection

We Need One Another

*Let us consider one another in order to
stir up love and good works.*
—HEBREWS 10:24

Scripture Reading: Hebrews 10:19-25

*W*hy go to church? We live in such a fast-paced society that we often have difficulty finding time for another activity. We have so many things to do on a weekend that there's just not enough time for church. When adults have full-time jobs along with all the other responsibilities of being spouses and parents, it's tough to allocate time for God.

We have found that the church provides a wonderful support group to help us live our life. During Emilie's recent bout with cancer, our strongest prayer supports came from our church family. They were the ones who offered meals, drove Emilie to doctors' appointments, helped us with our office work, ran errands, and, above all, supported us in prayer.

Banding together can provide the stimulus and solid foundation that helps us get through life's difficulties. If we attempt to do it by ourselves, we often fail. Someone who comes alongside us gives extra incentive to stick to our program, whether it be dieting, studying, exercise, praying, or encouraging our spouses and children. Together we can conquer and accomplish amazing things for God's kingdom.

Action

> Where do you need someone alongside to help you? Reach out to others and build strong relationships.

Prayer

> *Father God, help us prioritize our lives so we have time to reach out and include those people who will stir up love and good works among us. Amen.*

Reflection

In the Garden

*Mary Magdalene came and told the disciples
that she had seen the Lord....*
—JOHN 20:18

Scripture Reading: John 20:11-18

As a young boy of nine, I experienced one of my favorite bonding moments with my grandfather on my father's side. He was a robust cotton farmer with hands of steel, and armor for battle, and a heart for God. Every Sunday morning while we would visit our "Papa," he would take us to Anderson Chapel Methodist Church on the outskirts of Anson, Texas. As we began to sing, Papa's rough voice would utter these words, "I come to the garden alone, while the dew is still on the roses, and the voice I hear falling on my ear, the Son of God discloses. And He walks with me, and He talks with me, and He tells me I am His own; and the joy we share as we tarry there, none other has ever known."

I will always remember this great scene. It made such an impression on a young boy's heart that it has stayed with me for more than five decades.

This great gospel song, "In the Garden," was written by C. Austin Miles in 1912 after reading the Scripture we used for today's passage. On that first Sunday morning after Christ's crucifixion, while it was still dark, Mary Magdalene quietly made her way to the tomb. As she noticed the stone had been rolled away and the tomb was empty she heard the risen Lord gently call her name. Mary was so touched that she replied, "Rabboni" [teacher].

Quite often as I work in my own garden in the cool of the morning before the noonday heat arrives, I catch myself singing the words to this beautiful hymn. The words and melody are so soothing to my spirit. I know without a doubt that God walks with me, and He talks with me, and He tells me I am His own.

Action

Go to your garden alone while the dew is still on the roses. While there, pray to God.

Prayer

Father God, thanks for the positive memories of childhood. And thank You for the music that has played such an important role in my understanding of the gospel. Amen.

Reflection

Why Are We So Different?

For You formed my inward parts;
You covered me in my mother's womb.
—PSALM 139:13

Scripture Reading: Psalm 139:13-18

*I*f you have been married for any length of time, you realize that your mate is certainly different from yourself. You may often ask, "Why can't he [or she] be like me?" The saying around our house is: "Men are weird, and wives are strange." That is so very true—and God designed us that way! We are in a real sense "prescription babies" in that God has a custom design for every individual, equipping each for specific achievement and purpose. The Lord has woven and knitted together our beings in the wombs of our mothers.

Men and women are dissimilar in many ways, including physiology and anatomy, thought patterns, cultural roles, height, weight, strength, compassion, and emotional expression. For the most part, these differences are the result of God's design. Genesis 1:27 reads, "So God created man in His own image; in the image of God He created him; male and female He created them." And God called His creation good. We get a glimpse of God's marvelous plan in human creation. Men and women, though very different, are made in God's image.

As a couple, we can move into our marriage relationship with the confidence that God has put each partner on the earth for a special purpose. As loving mates, our task is to investigate to see what that purpose is and then do all we can to encourage and assist our mates so they can become all that God has planned for them.

We have a choice: We can live in war zones fueled by conflict and frustration or we can live in homes filled with the precious and pleasant riches that come from understanding and accepting our differences (see Proverbs 24:4).

Action

Begin to embrace your differences. Talk about them. And stop trying to change your partner

Prayer

Father God, we want to break down our walls of pride so we can enjoy all the differences You have created in us. Amen.

Reflection

A Few Small Words

Your sins are forgiven.
—LUKE 7:48

Scripture Reading: Luke 7:36-50

*P*ower oftentimes comes in small packages. Sometimes people of slight stature are much stronger than people twice their size. Many great leaders of our world have spoken words that have stirred souls, directed nations, healed spirits, and lifted hopes. But none of these utterances have had a greater impact than this little sentence: "Your sins are forgiven." It is so short, yet it has the power to change all of mankind for eternity.

This powerful forgiveness was not granted to a queen or to the wife of a great president. Jesus said it to a low-down sinner—who happened to be a woman. The culture of that day classified her as a second-rate member of the community. Worse yet, she was a woman with a bad reputation. Very few people would have invited her into their homes for dinner. But Jesus chose to speak to this very simple woman with a message of love: "Your sins are forgiven!" This declaration exhibits the abundant grace from Jesus, the Son of God who came to forgive all of our sins. No other person in history can make such a proclamation. Jesus is the only person so qualified. This is the biggest little sentence ever uttered!

We're so glad that Jesus said these words to this woman because we, too, can receive this same forgiveness for our sins—and so can you. Don't be concerned if your sins are as big as this lady's sins. No matter where you stand in the depths of sin, Jesus is able to forgive you all of your trespasses.

Action

If your sins have never been forgiven, ask God to forgive them today.

Prayer

Father God, we come to You as sinners and ask for Your forgiveness. Be merciful to us. Give us your peace today. Amen.

Reflection

Giving More Than a Song or Dance

*Go therefore and make disciples of all the nations,
baptizing them in the name of the Father and
of the Son and of the Holy Spirit.*

—MATTHEW 28:19

Scripture Reading: Matthew 28:16-20

During World War II, a commanding officer sent for his chaplain. "Chaplain, in three hours, half my men will be dead. We have been ordered to advance into what seems like certain annihilation. The men have been notified. They are nervous and perhaps more than a little afraid. Speak to them for me."

The chaplain hesitated only for a moment. Finding a place from which he could be seen and heard, he called for their attention. "Men," he shouted, "the colonel has told you of the impending attack. You know what lies ahead. But now, for a little while, let's forget that. Let me entertain you. What would you like? A song? A dance? A funny story?"

There was a long pause, then one soldier raised his hand in the air. "Yes, what will it be, son?"

"If that's all you've got to offer us, sir, I don't reckon it makes any difference."

We need to offer people more than a song, a dance, or a funny story when they so desperately need to hear the way of salvation. We are accountable by the blessings we have received. We are accountable by the way we live. Our lives must point to Jesus Christ.

Action

Be prepared to share more than a song, a dance, or a funny story.

Prayer

Father God, prepare our hearts and minds with the knowledge necessary to help someone accept Christ as his or her personal Savior. Amen.

Reflection

A Deceptive Life

Even so you also outwardly appear righteous to men, but
inside you are full of hypocrisy and lawlessness.
—MATTHEW 23:28

Scripture Reading: Matthew 23:23-28

There was an old man in town named "Grandpa Hicks," who made his living by deceptive means. He trapped fish illegally in a lake near his home. He rented out boats that didn't belong to him and pocketed the money. He stole gasoline for his motorboat from boats at a neighboring dock. And he would steal catfish from the lines of other anglers. He seemed to have no conscience about such matters. One Sunday morning two of his grandchildren asked if he'd take them fishing. With great conviction he replied, "I never fish on Sundays. I wasn't brought up like that."

Do we place a greater value on the legalistic observance of a certain day than on a holy life? A very good friend of ours related a business encounter with a member of our church. While doing business with the gentleman, he couldn't believe the inconsistency between the Sunday Christian he thought he knew and the business Christian. Our friend inquired about this confusion, and the Sunday Christian said that what he did at his business Monday through Saturday had no bearing on what he did on Sunday. How sad that a man could act one way one day and do the opposite on the next day—and not see the flaw in his 24-hours-a-day, 7-days-a-week walk with His Lord.

Action

Make sure that your Monday through Saturday walk is the same as your Sunday profession.

Prayer

Father God, we want our walk with You to be consistent every day. Amen.

Reflection

~~~~~~~~~~~~

Hold fast the time! Guard it, watch over it, every hour, every minute! Unregarded it slips away, like a lizard, smooth, slippery. Hold every moment sacred. Give each clarity and meaning, each the weight of thine awareness, each its true and due fulfillment.

—THOMAS MANN

~~~~~~~~~~~~

From Ugliness to Glory

We beheld His glory, the glory as of the only begotten of the Father, full of grace and truth.
—JOHN 1:14

Scripture Reading: John 1:14-18

*E*ach day when we open our newspaper, view the news on television, or hear the latest updates on the radio, we see and hear of ugliness:

- Families are killed by drunk drivers
- Senior citizens are duped out of their savings
- Crime runs rampant in our communities
- Wars break out
- A teenager shoots and kills fellow students
- There are people starving all over the world
- Abortion is common
- Divorce shatters the hopes of families

Malice is everywhere. We don't have to look very far to find evil. But due to Jesus' coming into the world, we are also able to see His glory abound! Because of what He did on the cross, we witness:

- Where there is sin—Jesus brings grace

- Where there is guilt—Jesus provides pardon

- Where there is depravity—Jesus brings cleansing

- Where there is sickness—Jesus brings healing

- Where there is no hope—Jesus brings new hope

When we get down because of the bad news all around us, we can look upward and see our God's love and provision.

It is easy to understand how excited the angels were when they appeared at the time of Jesus' birth and shouted, "Glory to God in the highest" (Luke 2:14). It was a new proclamation given to an ugly world. The last 2000 years have been a revelation of God's impact on society through the glory of His Son, Jesus. Where would we be today if Jesus had not intervened?

Action

Look around and discover the majesty of God. Jot down what you see and discuss them with your spouse before going to sleep tonight.

Prayer

Father God, truly You are a God of glory. Let our eyes look upward when things look so bad down here. Thank You for Your shining love. Amen.

Reflection

Be a Student of Your Children

Train up a child in the way he should go, and when he is old he will not depart from it.

—Proverbs 22:6

Scripture Reading: Proverbs 22:1-16

Today's passage has caused a lot of heartache in godly parents who have loved and cherished their children. As they have grown up, some of the children have drifted from their parents first love—God. How can this be? Isn't this verse in Proverbs one of God's promises to us as parents?

Generally speaking wise parents do produce wise children. There are exceptions. God has given every individual the freedom to choose his or her own way.

In the setting of the time this was written, "train up" meant to put something into the mouth. In Solomon's time, this term was used to describe the way a midwife, after delivering the child, would dip her fingers into crushed dates and massage the gums of the newborn with her sweet-tasting fingers to stimulate sucking. Then, when placed at the mother's breast, the infant would begin to feed.

The phrase "in the way" suggests to some "God's way" or "the path of wisdom"; others believe the phrase is a call for parents to discover the child's natural bent or characteristics and interests.

We have tried with our own two children and five grandchildren to figure out how uniquely God has made them. He has helped us understand that children need to be trained in a way that's tailor-made for them personally.

As parents we are to continue training our children as long as they are under our care. We are to train our children God's way, not according to our own ideas, our own ways, or our own plans. We must be students of each child if we are to know him or her individually. What may be true of one child might not be true of the others.

Action

Become students of each of your children. Take an 8½" x 11" sheet of paper and write the name of each child at the top (one page for each child). Journal their unique features.

Prayer

Father God, thank You for each child You have given us. Help us to know each of them well. Amen.

Reflection

Living Through a Terrible Day

But let us who are of the day be sober, putting on the breast-plate of faith and love, and as a helmet the hope of salvation.
—1 THESSALONIANS 5:8

Scripture Reading: 1 Thessalonians 5:1-11

Not too many years ago, a children's book by Judith Viorst appeared on the market and became an instant classic. It was called *Alexander and the Terrible, Horrible, No Good, Very Bad Day*. We all know what it's like to have that kind of awful day.

"In this world you will have trouble, " Jesus told us. That means we all have our quota of "terrible, horrible, no good, very bad" days. And that's not even counting the "stop everything" kind of bad days when we sit at a death bed, get legal papers, or hear a negative diagnosis.

Bad days are a given in this fallen world, so we might as well expect them. But can we find hope in them? One of two things is true about every bad day of our lives: Either we will live through it and be given a chance at another day... and that's reason for hope or we won't live through it, and we will have the opportunity to spend eternity with a heavenly Father who loves us. That, too, is reason for hope.

We serve a God of new beginnings. The hope He offers us is fresh every morning. We can end our terrible, horrible, no good, very bad days with the expectation that God always has something better for us. Thank God for His hope-giving grace on awful days. Ask for the strength and courage to endure it.[6]

Action

On difficult days, ask God if He has something for you to learn.

Prayer

Father God, we know that hope grows in a variety of circumstances, including rotten days. Give us the wisdom we need to get through the hard times. Amen.

Reflection

Blessed Assurance

*For God so loved the world that He gave His only begotten
Son, that whoever believes in Him should not perish
but have everlasting life.*
—JOHN 3:16

Scripture Reading: John 3:1-21

*Blessed assurance, Jesus is mine!
O what a foretaste of glory divine!
Heir of salvation, purchase of God,
Born of His Spirit, washed in His blood*

*This is my story, this is my song,
Praising my Savior all the day long.
This is my story, this is my song,
Praising my Savior all the day long.*

Generations of church-goers have sung these words written by Fanny Crosby,* but how many of us have the blessed assurance of salvation? Queen Victoria of England was one person who didn't. One day, after an especially moving service at St. Paul's Cathedral in London, she asked her chaplain if one could be absolutely sure of going to heaven. He told her he knew of no way. How tragic not to know!

*Music written by Phoebe Palmer Knapp, 1873.

News of this conversation reached the ears of a humble gospel minister by the name of John Townsend, who wrote a letter to the queen. He told her that the Bible is clear that we can be certain, for God does not want us to go through life with doubts about where we will spend eternity. Mr. Townsend gave her three Scriptures as proof of that assurance. One was John 3:16 and the other two were Romans 3:23: "For all have sinned and fall short of the glory of God" and 1 Peter 3:18: "For Christ also suffered once for sins, the just for the unjust, that He might bring us to God." Through His death and resurrection, Jesus Christ, God's Son, has paid the penalty for our sins so that we can be restored to fellowship with God and know we'll experience everlasting life with Him in heaven.

Pastor Townsend closed his letter to the queen by quoting, Romans 10:9: "If you confess with your mouth the Lord Jesus and believe in your heart that God has raised Him from the dead, you will be saved."

In her reply, Queen Victoria told Pastor Townsend that she now believed in the finished work of Christ for her and was looking forward to meeting Him in heaven.

Action
> Sing together the song "Blessed Assurance."

Prayer
> *Father God, we commit our lives to others so they may have the blessed assurance of knowing You as their personal Savior. Amen.*

Reflection

Do Business Till I Come

Why then did you not put my money in the bank?
—LUKE 19:23

Scripture Reading: Luke 19:11-27

Many of us have come into adulthood with very little training in wise money management. Often we enter into marriage with very poor habits regarding the proper use of God's resources. In order to have good financial planning, we must understand that this is part of wise stewardship. To be good stewards, we must believe that the money being managed belongs to someone else—God! When we have this point of view, we have the freedom to use financial resources as a tool to accomplish God's purposes.

God has entrusted each of us with certain resources, and we will be accountable for how we used His resources (Luke 19:11-26). Throughout Scripture we are given basic principles for handling God's provisions:

- Everything belongs to God (Psalm 24:1).

- Avoid an overly consumptive lifestyle—moderation is the fashion (1 Corinthians 9:25).

- Stay out of debt (Proverbs 22:7; Romans 13:8).

- Develop a plan to save (Proverbs 12:11).

- Plan long-term goals (Proverbs 13:22)

Many experts in the field of marriage indicate that money problems are one of the main factors of divorce. It's important to reduce the stresses that improper handling of money can cause. Spend time gathering information about the proper care of money. There are many resources available from books, magazines, videos, Internet chat rooms, and seminars. Work on your money issues together. Help each other grow in financial savvy. Don't be afraid to discuss priorities, viewpoints, and guidelines for day-to-day money dealings.

Action
Recognize that every resource belongs to God.

Prayer
Father God, we want to be faithful and be good stewards of all Your resources. We want to be Your servant; help us get on top of this area in our marriage. Amen.

Reflection

Hurry Up, Lord!

*Delight yourself also in the LORD, and He shall
give you the desires of your heart.*
—PSALM 37:4

Scripture Reading: Psalm 37:1-8

D o you find yourself wanting to hurry up God? We know He hears, but His answers are sometimes too slow. We need a 9:30 A.M. answer, and it doesn't come then. We've certainly wished that God was on our timetable. In our impatience we want to say, "Hurry up!"

Since we are victims of the hurry-up, throw-away world preoccupied with our own agenda, today's Scripture is especially relevant. Its theme is: "Trust in the LORD, and do good; dwell in the land, and feed on His faithfulness....Commit your way to the LORD, trust also in Him, and He shall bring it to pass....Rest in the LORD and wait patiently for Him; do not fret" (Psalm 37:3,5,7). The key elements to becoming free from hurry–hurry–hurry are to emphasize:

- Trust—and do good.
- Dwell—and cultivate faithfulness.
- Rest—and wait patiently.
- Fret not—lean on the Lord.

God promises to act *when* we obey His instructions and *commit our ways* to Him. He keeps His promises according to His timetable—not ours. The words in Psalm 37:1-8 encourage our hurry-up spirits to grow in trust and obedience as we live life in expectancy of God's certain actions on our behalf.

Action

Wait on the Lord today!

Prayer

Father God, in our lives of impatience please help us learn to trust, dwell, rest, and fret not. We want to be better equipped to accept Your timetable for our lives. Amen.

Reflection

~~~~~~~~

Live neither in the past nor in the future, but let each day's work absorb your entire energies, and satisfy your wildest ambition.

—WILLIAM OSLER

~~~~~~~~

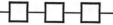

Know the Fear
of God

Fear Him who is able to destroy both soul and body.
—MATTHEW 10:28

Scripture Reading: Matthew 10:24-33

---

*S*ome Christians are very fearful of all kinds of events and situations. For instance, the Y2K threat embroiled the church in controversy. People were asking: What do we do? How should we act? Do we sell off our homes and investments? Should we stock up on cash, food, and water?

Fear robs us of confidence and joy and tarnishes our effectiveness in serving God. How are we to act when earthly fears show up? Peter counseled, "Who is going to harm you if you are eager to do good? But even if you should suffer for what is right, you are blessed. 'Do not fear what they fear'...but in your hearts set apart Christ as Lord" (1 Peter 3:13-15 NIV).

We are to turn to our Lord and Savior for strength, comfort, and wisdom in times of trouble and uncertainty. In Psalm 27 the writer shares the heart of coping with fear:

> The LORD is my light and my salvation; whom shall I fear? The LORD is the strength of my life; of

whom shall I be afraid?...One thing I have desired of the LORD, that will I seek: that I may dwell in the house of the LORD all the days of my life, to behold the beauty of the LORD and to inquire in His temple (verses 1,4).

Action

Examine what your fears are. Ask God to help you conquer your fears and rest completely in Him.

Prayer

Father God, help us distinguish the differences in the types of fears we have. We want to trust You in all things. Amen.

Reflection

Run Away from Evil

Flee also youthful lusts.
—2 TIMOTHY 2:22

Scripture Reading: 2 Timothy 2:14-26

I could really be a strong Christian if I could
_____." We all can identify with that plea.
Satan knows our weak areas of life and he
hammers at us like pounding waves during a hurricane.
He attempts to break down the very heart of our lives—
our relationship with God. How can we withstand this
continual bombardment? Here's one suggestion:

> Little Jeff was trying his best to save enough
> money to buy his mother a present. It was a terrible
> struggle because he gave in so easily to the
> temptation to buy goodies from the ice cream man
> whenever the brightly colored van came through
> the neighborhood.
>
> One night after his mother had tucked him
> into bed, she overheard him praying, "Please, dear
> God, help me to run away when the ice cream man
> comes down our street tomorrow."

Even at his young age, Jeff had learned that one of the
best ways to overcome temptation is to stay away from
it. In 1 Corinthians 10:13 we read, "No temptation has

overtaken you except such as is common to man; but God is faithful, who will not allow you to be tempted beyond what you are able, but with the temptation will also make the way to escape, that you may be able to bear it." Even with this promise, we must be willing to do our part. Many times that involves avoiding situations that would contribute to our spiritual defeat.

How many times do we read in the newspapers about people who have terrible things happen to them because they were in the wrong place at the wrong time. We should be on guard and never let ourselves be in the wrong places or with people who will try to lead us into sin.

Action

Flee from your youthful lusts. Say no to Satan.

Prayer

Father God, help us be quick to run away from the ice cream man or other dangers. Amen.

Reflection

Petitions for Our Children

You shall teach them diligently to your children, and shall talk of them when you sit in your house, when you walk by the way, when you lie down, and when you rise up.

—DEUTERONOMY 6:7

Scripture Reading: Deuteronomy 6:1-9

---

*M*oses directed the Israeli nation to do everything possible to remember the commands (the sum and substance of the law) and to incorporate them into everyday life. Part of this included the spiritual education of the children. In Hebrew the word for "parent" is teacher. Spiritual teaching would take place daily through the study of God's Word, the reputation of the Law, and the examples the parents exhibited in their lives. The instruction was more than just the reading and memorization of the law—it included the demonstration of a godly lifestyle woven into everyday living.

Parents have to be creative in the ways they teach. We need to be alert to life and the events that are happening around us. Use the news to point out examples of good and evil. The seasonal holidays are great opportunities to evaluate the origins of each one. Anniversaries, birthdays, weddings, funerals, and new births are perfect times to instruct your children in God's laws. Strolling on the beach, hiking, sleeping out under the stars, cooking together, or working on a car can be a treasured moment to teach truths.

As parents, we are always teaching—which is different than lecturing. Remain open to questions. Watch your nonverbal language when shocking comments come forth. Pray for wisdom, guidance, and patience before and during your times with your children.

Action

Become aware of the teaching challenge that is before you as parents. Discuss how you will begin or continue in this important endeavor.

Prayer

Father God, we are in awe at what it takes to raise godly children. Continue to give us the desire to be Your servants in this area of our lives. Give us wisdom and guidance. Amen.

Reflection

Who Is the Focus of Your Life?

I also count all things loss for the excellence of the knowledge of Christ Jesus my Lord.
—PHILIPPIANS 3:8

Scripture Reading: Philippians 3:1-11

We don't know about you, but we've never met a grandmother who at the drop-of-a-hat couldn't pull from her purse a gallery of pictures of her grandchildren. They usually extend from birth to the current school photo. Talk, talk, talk—all they want to talk about is their grandchildren. There is an old saying among grandparents that states, "If we would have known how much fun grandchildren are, we would have had them first." We talk freely about those things we love.

Ray Stedman, the late pastor of Peninsula Bible Church in Palo Alto, CA, developed the concept in church worship called "Body Life." He told of a little boy who was asked by his mother how his Sunday school class had gone that morning. The boy said, "Oh, we had a new teacher. Guess who she was?" "Who?" she replied. "It was Jesus' grandmother," he informed her. Amused, she asked, "What made you think that?" The boy answered, "Well, all she did was show us pictures of Jesus and tell us stories about Him."

We talk most about what or who is important to us. Is Jesus a main topic of conversation in your life? Do others sense how important He is to you?

Action

What percent of your talking revolves around Jesus? Do you need to reevaluate your priorities?

Prayer

Father God, continue to give us the desire to know You more. We want You to be the center of our lives. Amen.

Reflection

~~~~~~~~~

God's love is so delightful—
any other pleasure seems
dismal in comparison with it.

—St. Catherine of Genoa

~~~~~~~~~

A Companion of Jesus

They realized that they had been with Jesus.
—ACTS 4:13

Scripture Reading: Acts 4:13-22

We often wonder if people around us know we are companions of Jesus. Do our neighbors, people at work, and our friends know from our presence that we love Jesus?

While staying at the University of Washington Medical Center, we became very attached to a young nurse who spent a lot of time caring for Emilie. We found ourselves talking to her about very personal things, including sharing with her the part that our faith had in our optimism toward Emilie's healing. Many times the nurse would wave, touch, or get teary-eyed when discussing her life. One late afternoon at her shift change and the beginning of a four-day-off schedule, she came into our room to say goodbye because we would be going to an out-patient status. As she came into the room she said, "I don't know why I'm attracted to you both, but you have something magnetic that most other patients don't have. I don't know what it is, but I like to be around you." Without hesitation Emilie responded with, "What you are seeing in us is Jesus!" This young nurse exited the room, went down the elevator, got onto her bicycle (a lot of people travel to and from work on their bicycles in Seattle), and rode off for a four-day break in her schedule knowing that she had been with companions of Jesus.

We are the salt of the earth, seasoning the world around us. People around us should sense that passages from the Bible have impacted our lives. We are to be different from the rest of the world. What "magic" did the nurse see in us?

- We were kind.

- We listened to her life story.

- We shared our faith and Scriptures that gave us hope for healing and for life.

- We exhibited a sweet, respectful spirit toward her, including saying "thank you" and "please."

- We shared our story of love for each other as a man and a woman who have been married nearly 45 years.

- We shared Jesus when appropriate.

Not every person we meet will be attracted to our Jesus, but the ones who are will be affected for the rest of their lives because we have revealed our companionship with Jesus.

Action
Reach out and touch someone's life today.

Prayer
Father God, give us someone today that we may touch his or her life by sharing our faith. Give us a love for people. Amen.

Reflection

An Unlikely Servant

The LORD has sought for Himself a man after His own heart.
—1 SAMUEL 13:14

Scripture Reading: 1 Samuel 2:1-7

Why would God choose a man like David to lead His people? Why does God call David, even after his disobedience, a man of God?

At various times in his life, David's actions revealed an attitude of self-sufficiency and pride. What redeemed him in God's eyes? In 2 Samuel 24:10, David made a great confession after he realized that he was wrong in asking for a census. He cried out, "I have sinned greatly." Through this confession he turned from his own sufficiency to God's sufficiency.

David became thirsty for God and His demand for obedience. He was quick to confess his sins and willing to repent. That's why he was a man after God's own heart. He had a heart for God, and that's what God looks for in our own hearts.

Action

Confess any known sin in your life, then move forward toward pleasing God.

Prayer

Father God, we give you our hearts. Use us! Amen.

Reflection

~~~~~~~~~~~~

*If we are depending on God, we
move closer to that beautiful picture
He wants to paint to the world
through us. We move closer to Him
and we learn to follow Him better.
Lord you are with me.*

—GLENN BAXLEY, EMILIE BARNES

~~~~~~~~~~~~

Planned Neglect

He knelt down on his knees three times that day,
and prayed and gave thanks before his God, as was
his custom since early days.

—DANIEL 6:10

Scripture Reading: Daniel 6:10-17

*A*re you the kind of person who puts off important actions because there are other, seemingly more important things to do? One of the disciplines that continually must be reinforced is spending time with the Lord on a consistent basis. We often say we want to begin the day in prayer and Scripture reading, but there are so many other things that get in the way: making the beds, picking up dirty clothes, starting the washing machine, mowing the lawn, cleaning the gutters, education, working, career goals. Soon we find ourselves at midday, and we haven't spent time with our Lord.

There was a noted concert violinist who was asked the secret of her mastery of the instrument. The woman answered the question with two words: "Planned neglect." Then she explained, "There were many things that used to demand my time. When I went to my room after breakfast, I made my bed, straightened the room, dusted, and did whatever seemed necessary. When I finished my work, I turned to my violin practice. That system prevented me from accomplishing what I should on the violin. So I reversed things. I deliberately planned to neglect everything else until my practice period was complete. And that program of planned neglect is the secret of my success."

If we don't do the most important things in our lives, we will let little things interrupt our focus. We shouldn't give God our leftover time when we're tired and hurried; God deserves first place in our lives.

Action
Make it a priority to walk with God early today.

Prayer
Father God, we don't want to give You second best. If we need to, we will get up 30 minutes earlier to spend time with You. Amen.

Reflection

What Keeps Me Alive

For to me, to live is Christ, and to die is gain.
—PHILIPPIANS 1:21

Scripture Reading: Philippians 3:1-11

*M*r. Jones experienced a very rough sea crossing. He became deathly ill and thought he would surely die. At a particularly rough time, a sea steward patted Mr. Jones on the shoulder and said, "I know, sir, that it seems awful, but remember, no man ever died of seasickness." Mr. Jones lifted his head, looking eye-to-eye with the steward, and replied, "Man, don't say that! It's only the wonderful hope of dying that keeps me alive."

Yes, the wonderful hope of dying kept Paul going. It wasn't the anticipation of stopping the suffering he was experiencing, but the ultimate realization that he would be with his heavenly Father.

We have experienced this same hope in our lives. During this battle with cancer, today's Scripture gave us purpose to go on. We continued to write our books not knowing if they would be completed or not. It gave us meaning every moment. It gave us a reason to live for Christ, yet, with the assurance that ultimately we will be with Christ in heaven.

Action

What would you do today if you knew this would be your last day on earth? Do it.

Prayer

Father God, thank You for the risen Christ—our reason for living. Amen.

Reflection

Lord,

Make me an instrument of Thy peace;
where there is hatred, let me sow love;
where there is injury, pardon; where
there is doubt, faith; where there is
despair, hope; where there is darkness,
light; where there is sadness, joy.

—St. Francis of Assisi

A Time to Laugh

*To everything there is a season...a time
to weep, and a time to laugh.*
—ECCLESIASTES 3:1,4

Scripture Reading: Ecclesiastes 3:1-13

I remember very vividly my father doubling up with laughter when we would watch the Three Stooges, Abbott & Costello, and Dean Martin and Jerry Lewis perform. He laughed so hard that we feared he would faint. A few years ago, as we were planning our goals for the next year, we made this entry on our planning sheets: *"We are to laugh more."*

Recent studies have shown that people who laugh a lot live longer. As Christians, we need to let Christ's joy spill over into happy laughter. There are other pluses when we laugh: our diaphragm goes down, our lungs expand, and we take in two or three times more oxygen than usual. This results in a surge of energy running through our bodies.

The medical profession states that few of us realize the health value we receive from laughing. Happy individuals recover from disease much more quickly than sad, complaining patients. A six-year-old girl had a very stern father who was very solemn and legalistic. One time when he took her to visit a farm, she was especially impressed with the family's pet horse. "Oh, horsey," she said in awe, "you must be a very good Christian. You have such a long face!"

We once had the opportunity to share the Lord with a public official in our community. After he had become a believer and active in our church, he gave testimony to the fact that one thing that had appealed to him and his wife was that they never knew Christians could have so much fun. Even though we worship a God who is holy, we must not forget the joy He gives us. Proverbs 17:22 states, "A merry heart does good, like medicine." As a couple, be known for your cheery smiles and attitudes.

Action

Make sure that today will be a day with laughter.

Prayer

Father God, let those around us see our joy. Let us be known as a couple who smiles. Amen.

Reflection

Be a Bed Carrier

He said to the man who was paralyzed, "I say to you, arise, take up your bed, and go to your house."
—LUKE 5:24

Scripture Reading: Luke 5:17-26

The sick man couldn't walk, so his friends carried him on his own bed. When the group arrived at the house where Jesus was teaching, they saw a large crowd of people. They couldn't even get close to Jesus for the healing of their friend. So, being creative, they carried their friend to the rooftop, cut a hole in the roof, and lowered the man in his bed to Jesus below. You can imagine the amazement Jesus and those in the crowd experienced when they saw a man and bed being lowered through the roof.

Jesus looked at the man who had come down through the roof and his friends above. "When He saw their faith, He said to him, 'Man, your sins are forgiven you.'" The sick man was obedient; he rose and walked. Throughout Scripture we are commanded to be obedient (see Acts 5:29; Daniel 7:27; 1 John 2:3,4). If we are to become all God wants us to be, we must be willing to go forth in faith and follow Jesus—even when we might not feel like it.

Action

Is God asking you to be obedient in an area of your life? If so, heed His call.

Prayer

Father God, may we be caring friends willing to help people hear Jesus so they can be healed of their sins. Amen.

Reflection

~~~~~~~~

Do all the good you can,
By all the means you can,
In all the ways you can,
In all the places you can,
At all the times you can,
To all the people you can,
As long as you can.
—JOHN WESLEY

~~~~~~~~

God Never Forgets

*Can a woman forget her nursing child, and not
have compassion on the son of her womb? Surely they
may forget, yet I will not forget you.*
—ISAIAH 49:15

Scripture Reading: Isaiah 49:14-18

Often we live in a world of fear—fear that we aren't worthy, fear that we won't get what we need, or fear that we won't get enough. Whatever the reason, fear and panic can build until hope seems to disappear. How do we stop this endless cycle? One way is to pay a little extra attention to giving your soul what it needs—and what it needs most of all is some quiet time with God. Open your heart and let God meet your needs. He's a loving Father. He wants to hold you in His arms, nurture you, care for you, and help you grow. He wants, more than anyone else in this entire world, to give you hope. Francis de Sales wrote:

> Do not look forward to the changes of this life
> in fear, rather look to them with full hope that, as
> they arise, God, whose you are, will deliver you
> out of them. He has kept you hitherto—do you but
> hold fast to his dear hand and he will lead you
> safely through all things; and when you cannot

stand, he will bear you in his arms. Do not look forward to what may happen tomorrow; the same everlasting Father who cares for you today will take care of you tomorrow, and every day. Either he will shield you from suffering, or he will give you unfailing strength to bear it. Be at peace, then, and put aside all anxious thoughts and imaginations.

Action

Believe that God will take care of every situation.

Prayer

Father God, help us cast all our anxieties on You because we know You care for us. Amen.

Reflection

Pruning Hurts

Every branch that bears fruit He prunes,
that it may bear more fruit.
—JOHN 15:2

Scripture Reading: John 15:1-8

---

*B*ob is a real believer in pruning all our trees and shrubs each year. I can't stand to go outside on those days. For 45 years I have said something like, "Bob, you are killing the plants. They will never grow back." For 45 years Bob has replied, "Emilie, you wait and see. In a few weeks the plants will be more beautiful than before." And you know what? For 45 years the plants have come back more beautiful than before.

Throughout Palestine vines grow abundantly, and every year gardeners prune the branches in order to produce high-quality fruit. Branches are considered useless unless they produce. Fruitless vines are drastically cut back, and the pruned limbs are destroyed. The Old Testament pictures Israel as the vineyard of God, so the vine became a symbol for the people of God. Jesus called Himself the true vine, using the vine and branches as an analogy to show how a believer must abide in Him. Jesus' followers who believed in Him were the branches on

God's vine. The branches had no source of life within themselves, but they received life from the vine. Without the vine, the branches could produce no fruit.

Perhaps, at times, you feel like a shrub being pruned. You want to cry out, "Stop! I've had enough!" When you cry out, are you hearing God say, "I'm answering your prayers. The unnecessary, the unproductive, must be cut off from your life so that the fruit will appear. Pruning is necessary in nature, and it is necessary in your life as My child. Remember it is your God who is doing the pruning. Pruning is a painful process, but it does not last forever. One day your cut branches will sprout forth new growth and fruit will appear."

Action

Trust your Master Gardener when He is pruning your branches.

Prayer

Father God, let us listen to You when You are pruning our lives. Let us not yell stop, but look at the shears and know that You have our best in mind. We look forward to bearing new fruit. Amen.

Reflection

When Things Go Wrong

But He knows the way that I take; when He
has tested me, I shall come forth as gold.

—JOB 23:10

Scripture Reading: Job 23:1-12

---

*D*o you remember Job's story? He was an upright man of God who was blessed with wealth, children, and possessions. To prove that Job was a man of God, Satan was allowed to take Job's possessions—including his health. But even in the face of so much physical evidence against him, Job still clung to the belief that God was aware of what was happening and cared. God knew that Job was blameless and that he would arise from this calamity as gold.

Our friends Glen and Marilyn Heavilin know the kind of suffering Job knew. They have lost three sons—one in a crib death, one twin by pneumonia, and the second twin by a drunk driver. Glen and Marilyn were tested, but they have come through it like gold from a refiner's furnace. Today they use their experiences to glorify the name of Jesus. Did God know what He was doing when He chose the Heavilins? Of course. They are able to shine for Him. Their pain will never be gone, but they still go forth to minister to others.

Everyone experiences some kind of tragedy. It's not the specifics of the event that matters as much as how we handle it. Remember that Jesus knows your pain. He is *always* with you to help you get through the tough times.

Action

If you are being tested, reach out to God for strength and find a support group that can help you during this difficult time.

Prayer

Father God, help us come through this difficult period of our lives as gold. Amen.

Reflection

A Child of the King

*The Spirit Himself bears witness with our spirit
that we are children of God.*

—ROMANS 8:16

Scripture Reading: Romans 8:12-17

As believers, young or old, we are children of God. If we know and accept that truth we never have to ask, "Who are we?" We already know we are very special. In our family, we often tell our children and grandchildren that they are special because they are children of God.

Harriett Buell wrote the words for "A Child of the King" one Sunday morning while walking home from her Methodist church service. She sent her text to the *Northern Christian Advocate* magazine, and it was printed in the February 1, 1877, issue. John Sumner, a singer and school music teacher, saw the words and composed the music. The hymn has been widely used since then to remind believers who they really are—bearers of God's image and children of the King of kings (see Genesis 1:26; Titus 6:15). The chorus of this great hymn is: "I'm a child of the King, a child of the King: with Jesus my Savior, I'm a child of the King."[7]

As children of the heavenly kingdom, we can enjoy and possess the rich spiritual blessings that belong to us as heirs of God's riches:

- We have been justified and made acceptable to God (Romans 5:1).

- We have been adopted into God's royal family (Romans 8:16-17).

- We have been given citizenship in heaven (Philippians 3:20).

- We possess the indwelling Holy Spirit (1 Corinthians 6:19).

- We have been placed into the kingdom of the Son of God's love (Colossians 1:13).

Action

Go out today and act like a child of the King!

Prayer

Father God, what an awesome thought to think that we are Your heirs. Your sacrifice on the cross and our belief in that act has made us Your children. We thank You for writing our names on Your family tree. Amen.

Reflection

There's Dough in the Dough

Let nothing be done through selfish ambition or conceit, but in lowliness of mind let each esteem others better than himself.

—PHILIPPIANS 2:3

Scripture Reading: Philippians 2:1-4

Most of us realize that manners in our society are increasingly declining. There's a breakdown of esteeming others. As a selfish society there's an emphasis on "me." This concept is so against our Christian teachings of loving others and being humble. As parents, one of our primary tasks is to teach our children respect, humility, and how to honor others. Here's a great illustration to teach unselfishness:

> A rich baker sent for 20 of the poorest children in town. He said to them, "In this basket is a loaf of bread for each of you. Take one and come back every day, and I'll give you more." Immediately the youngsters began quarreling about who would get the largest loaf. Snatching them from the basket, they left without even thanking the baker.
>
> Sally, a poorly dressed little girl, patiently waited until the others had left. She then took the

smallest loaf, which remained in the basket, kissed the old man's hand, and went home. The next day the scene was repeated. But when Sally's mother sliced this loaf, she found many shiny silver pieces inside. When Sally took the money back to the baker, he said, "No, my child, it was not a mistake. I put them into the smallest loaf to reward you for your gentleness and unselfishness."

Action

Be willing to be unselfish for Jesus' sake. Go out today and esteem another person over your own self-interest.

Prayer

Father God, as we meet others today, give us hearts willing to edify others. May it start in our own home. Amen.

Reflection

Be a Lover
of God

Fulfill my joy by being like-minded, having the same love,
being of one accord, of one mind.
—PHILIPPIANS 2:2

Scripture Reading: Philippians 2:1-11

---

*F*riendship is the launching pad for every love and spills into the other important relationships of life. It is the beginning of all levels of intimacy—with our mates, with our parents, with our children, with everyone we encounter. When our son, Brad, was a young man beginning to date, we gave him one piece of advice for his future relationship with young women: "Be a friend going in, be a friend while dating, and remain a friend when you leave." As we look over his dating years, he must have followed our advice because so many of his ex-girlfriends often mention what a gentleman he was when they dated. We now have the opportunity to pass our advice on to our 15-year-old grandson, Chad.

Gentleness and sincerity are crucial to forming close bonds. In our seminars and speaking engagements, we often tell women that they need to share often with their husbands how to be soft and tender. Many men have never had a role model to show how to be a close friend and lover. And research points out that people with strong, supportive relationships live longer than the general population!

Action

Discuss with your spouse how you could be a better friend.

Prayer

Father God, we know we can't love others if we don't love You first, ourselves second, and other people third. Let us reach out and be friends to others. Amen.

Reflection

Servant Leadership

So God created man in His own image; in the image of God He created him; male and female He created them.

—GENESIS 1:27

Scripture Reading: Genesis 1:26-31

---

*I*n our society we struggle with who is going to lead the marriage and family. The secular world would have us believe that it is a democratic process built on voting and negotiating.

Headship, in Scripture, is very clear. This role is assigned to the man during the very act of creation. The man was created first and the woman was created as his helper. The wife from the very beginning was to fulfill three roles:

- Have fellowship with the man so he would not be alone.

- Continue the legacy of family by providing ancestry.

- Do the work assigned to her from God.

Marriage was designed by God to be a picture of the relationship between Christ and His church.

In biblical headship, the husband has the responsibility to exhibit true servanthood, be humble, and not act with prideful leadership in the home (see Ephesians 5:23-29). Our Lord exhibited such a pattern of leadership. He showed servanthood, but He still reflected leadership (see Luke 22:26; Hebrews 13:17).

The husband is to lead his family as a team that glorifies God. The husband serves his family to meet their needs in a loving and nourishing fashion. As men, we are to cherish our wives as treasures who have much value. As we serve our families, we will be moving forward in God's plan for us to have an orderly unit that reflects the love of Christ.

Action

Identify one person in your family whom you can serve today. Go out and do it.

Prayer

Father God, impress upon our hearts that we want to follow the biblical principle of being a servant to each other in our marriage. We want our lives to reflect the model that Your Scripture describes. Amen.

Reflection

Finding Purpose

Whatever a man sows, that he will also reap.
—GALATIANS 6:7

Scripture Reading: Galatians 6:6-10

The psalmist said it so very well when he wrote: "Those who wept as they went out carrying the seed will come back singing for joy, as they bring in the harvest" (Psalm 126:6 GNB). In order to have joy in our later years, we must endure the hardships and pain associated with the planting process. We have found it is very painful to plant seeds, but oh, the joy of enjoying the fruits of the harvest!

A wealthy noblewoman had grown tired of life. She had everything one could wish for except happiness and contentment. She said, "I am weary of life. I will go to the river and there end my life." As she walked along, she felt a little hand tugging at her skirt. Looking down, she saw a frail, hungry-looking little boy who pleaded, "There are six of us. We are dying for want of food!" The woman thought, *Why should I not relieve this wretched family? I have the means, and it seems I will have no more use for riches when I am gone.*

Following the little boy, she entered a scene of misery, sickness, and want. She opened her purse and emptied its contents. The family members were beside themselves with joy and gratitude. Even more taken aback with their needs, the noble lady said, "I'll return tomorrow, and I will share with you more of the good things God has given to me in abundance!"

Here was a noble lady who found one of the true meanings of life—giving herself to others! When we bring sunshine into the lives of others, we always receive back some of the rays.

Action

Spend time planting seeds today.

Prayer

Father God, we know that if we are to receive the joy of the harvest we must experience the weeping as we carry out the seed. Let us begin the work today. Amen.

Reflection

Salty Speech

You are the salt of the earth; but if the salt loses its flavor, how shall it be seasoned? It is then good for nothing.

—Matthew 5:13

Scripture Reading: Matthew 5:13-16

*L*iving in southern California, we spend a lot of time at the beach. Since childhood we have waded, paddled, surfed, and swam in salty water. We are surprised when out-of-state friends come with us to the beach for the first time. They're amazed that the water tastes salty and that it is easier to float in salt water. One might reason that salt water is salt water; however, if you were to evaporate a ton of water from the Pacific Ocean, you would get around 79 pounds of salt; from the Atlantic Ocean you would yield 81 pounds of salt; from the Dead Sea you would get almost 500 pounds of salt.

Obviously, the earth's bodies of water vary greatly in the amount of saltiness. Today's reading says that we are "the salt of the earth." But it seems like we have different levels of "salt content." Throughout Scripture we see that salt enhances flavor (Job 6:6); indicates purity in speech (Colossians 4:6); symbolizes keeping a promise (Numbers 18:19); refers to goodness (Mark 9:50).

We need to step back, look in a mirror, and see how much salt we have in our lives. Are others seasoned by being around us? Is our speech uplifting to those who need encouragment? Do our actions inspire those who are in our presence? Are our spouses closer to God because they are married to us? If we don't like what we see, we can ask God for more salt to flavor all that we do. He will hear our prayers and we can truly become the salt of the earth.

Action

Shake salt on someone today.

Prayer

Father God, if we have held back the salt from those we meet, let us be more generous with the seasoning You have given us. Let others be thirsty for You! Amen.

Reflection

Remember Me

Do this in remembrance of Me.
—1 CORINTHIANS 11:24

Scripture Reading: 1 Corinthians 11:23-34

---

*I*n the front of our church there is a communion table that has the following words carved in its front: "Do this in remembrance of Me." When Jesus told His disciples to participate in communion, or the Lord's Supper by breaking bread and drinking together, He wanted them to remember His death on the cross and anticipate His return in the future.

The bread reminds us that the second person of the Trinity became flesh and dwelt among us (John 1:14). He took our sins upon Himself and suffered the cross to cleanse us (1 Peter 2:24). The cup symbolizes the blood He shed (Matthew 26:28). We must be careful not to take the bread and cup in an unworthy manner (see 1 Corinthians 11:27). We are to examine ourselves *before* we participate in communion and repent of any wrongs we've committed. We are to remember Christ's sacrifice for us and confess our sins to God.

Likewise, when we touch our wedding rings may we use this time to remember when we were married. Hear again those words we uttered to our mates. Are there any sins that we can confess to God that would enrich our marriages?

Action

Mentally examine your hearts to see if you are still on course in carrying out your wedding vows. If there are areas in which you need strength, confess to God and ask for His help.

Prayer

Father God, we wish to ask Your forgiveness in how we have fallen short in keeping our wedding vows. We want to be better mates. Amen.

Reflection

~~~~~~~~~~

We are children of God, created by Him. He made us each beautiful in His sight. Make the effort to find that beauty in others. He encourages my soul.

—GLENN BAXLEY, EMILIE BARNES

~~~~~~~~~~

Know the Real

Take heed to yourself and to the doctrine.
—1 TIMOTHY 4:16

Scripture Reading: 1 Timothy 4:12-16

Scripture warns against false prophets and improper teachings. There are many people who might tickle our ears, but some will try to lead us astray. How can we detect false teaching? The solution is quite easy: Learn the truth so well that you'll be able to recognize errors the moment you read, see, or hear them. Here's a story that helps illustrate this point.

A boy who wanted to learn about jade went to study with a talented old teacher. This gentleman put a piece of the precious stone into the boy's hand and told him to hold it tight. Then he began to talk of philosophy, men, women, the sun, and almost everything under it. After an hour he took back the stone and sent the boy home. This same procedure was repeated for several weeks. The boy became very frustrated. When would he be told about jade? He was too polite, however, to question the wisdom of his teacher. Then one day, when the old man put a stone into his hands, the boy cried out, "That's not jade!" He had become so familiar with the genuine that he could immediately detect a counterfeit.

As believers we must study, hear, and talk of God's truth so we will immediately know when false truth is presented to us. We also need to pray for discernment. If a teaching isn't faithful to the Bible, the Holy Spirit will help us know there is an error presented.

Action

Listen, read, and hear with a more discerning mind and heart. Ask the Holy Spirit to help you detect false teachings.

Prayer

Father God, open our hearts so that we will examine what is presented to us and know when it is true or false. Amen.

Reflection

The Amazing Watermelon

*O LORD, how manifold are Your works! In wisdom You have
made them all. The earth is full of Your possessions.*
—PSALM 104:24

Scripture Reading: Psalm 104:24-30

As a young boy of nine, I went to my grandfather's farm in Texas to help with the chores. I would ride behind a team of mules to plow the ground after tending to the weeds that grew in the furrows. I fed the animals at night, picked up the eggs for morning breakfast, and picked cotton in season. During the heat of summer, we would get very hot and sweaty. One of our rewards was to go to the watermelon patch and break open a ripe melon. The juice ran all over, and this sweet refreshment gave us a great break in a very hard lifestyle. The watermelon is an amazing plant!

According to William Jennings Bryan, a famous American lawyer and creationist, a watermelon speaks volumes about God. Bryan wrote:

> Recently someone planted just one little seed in the ground. Under the influence of sunshine and rain, it took off its coat and went to work gathering about 200,000 times its own weight. It forced all that material through a tiny stem and built a

141

watermelon. On the outside it had a covering of green; within that, a rind of white; and within that, a core of red. Scattered on the inside were more seeds—each capable of doing the same work all over again.

There are many questions we can ask: "Who designed such a melon? How did the watermelon seed get so strong? How did the color and flavoring get inside the juicy melon?"

Bryan pointed out that until we can figure out the mysteries of the watermelon, how can we begin to understand the awesomeness of creation. We only have to look around to see the power of God revealed in all He has made.

As today's verse said, "O LORD, how manifold are Your works! In wisdom You have made them all."

Action

Acknowledge that God is the creator of everything—seen and unseen.

Prayer

Father God, we're awestruck by the works of Your hands. Thank You for creating us and the world we live in. Amen.

Reflection

Give Your Child a Good Name

And those who know Your name will
put their trust in You.
—PSALM 9:10

Scripture Reading: Psalm 9:9-12

Your Name

You got it from your father, 'twas the best he had
    to give.
And right gladly he bestowed it, it's yours the
    while you live.
You may lose the watch he gave you and another
    you may claim,
But remember, when you're tempted, to be careful
    of his name.

It was fair the day you got it, and a worthy name
    to bear,
When he took it from his father, there was no
    dishonor there.
Through the years he proudly wore it, to his father
    he was true,

143

And that name was clean and spotless when he
   passed it on to you.

Oh, there's much that he has given that he valued
   not at all.
He has watched you break your playthings in the
   days when you were small.
You have lost the knife he gave you, and you've
   scattered many a game,
But you'll never hurt your father if you're careful
   with his name.

It's yours to wear forever, yours to wear the while
   you live,
Yours perhaps, some distant morning, another boy
   to give.
And you'll smile as did your father—with a smile
   that all can share,
If a clean name and a good name you are giving
   him to wear.

—Edgar Guest

Action

Give your children every reason to be proud of
their name.

Prayer

*Father God, the legacy of a good name is so important to
a child. We want to pass on to our children a name they
can be proud of. Let us make good decisions today so
they can be proud of us tomorrow. Amen.*

Reflection

House Hunting

In My Father's house are many mansions....
I go to prepare a place for you.
—JOHN 14:2

Scripture Reading: John 13:33–14:4

---

*T*here are different passages a couple travels through life. We recently made the major decision to sell the "Barnes' Barn" after 16 years and move back to Newport Beach, California, where Emilie's oncologist practices medicine. It was a very tearful experience to leave our home after all these years, but we knew we couldn't keep up our property while we were concentrating on getting Emilie healed from cancer.

Looking for that new perfect home is another adventure. Each of us were drawn to different houses. Our realtors, bless their patience, kept showing us homes on the market. Then one day our sales rep called and said she had the perfect house to show us. It met all the qualifications on our wish list. Sure enough, it was just what we were looking for!

How thankful we are that, as Christians, we do not have this problem regarding our heavenly home. Jesus assures us that He has already located, purchased, and closed escrow on our mansion in heaven. He promises to take us there to be with His Father forever. What a comfort to know that when believing loved ones die they have moved into that perfect home made just for them. No "For Sale" signs on the lawn; they are ushered into their heavenly home to spend eternity with their Lord.

Action

Praise God for His heavenly provision for you and your family. Rest in the knowledge that you have a mansion on high.

Prayer

Father God, thank You for assuring us that You have gone before us and paid the price for our eternal salvation. We look forward to being with You in the heavenlies. Amen.

Reflection

Answer Nothing

But Jesus still answered nothing, so that Pilate marveled.
—MARK 15:5

Scripture Reading: Mark 15:1-5

We live in a world where everyone wants their rights. People argue to make others understand their reasonable positions. Even when guilty, criminals will answer back to the accusers "not guilty." When Jesus was brought before Pilate for judgment, Jesus kept His words clear and succinct. Pilate asked Jesus if He was the king of the Jews. Jesus responded, "It is as you say" (Mark 15:2). Even with other accusations, the Lord said nothing more.

There is a lot to learn from Jesus' choice to remain quiet. British writer Mrs. Jessie Penn-Lewis, commenting on the silence of Jesus, said that the Christian who is living close to the Lord will manifest humility and self-control under the most trying circumstance. She also advocated being silent in our lowly service among others, not seeking to be "seen of men." Be silent while we stoop to serve the very ones who betrayed us. Be silent when forced by others to some position where apparent rivalry with another much-abused servant of God seems imminent, followed by utter self-effacement in our withdrawal. Be silent when our words are misquoted.

Mrs. Lewis concluded with this prayer: "O Anointed Christ, the Lamb of God, You alone can live this life of silent, self-effacement in a world of self-assertion and self-love. Live this life in me."

If we could just practice the silence of Jesus before Pilate, we would improve our day-to-day relationships. We never have to say "I'm sorry" when we haven't said unnecessary words. Words once out of our mouths cannot be taken back. We don't have to insist on getting our rights. We don't have to puff up ourselves in order for others to know who we are or to know our opinions are right. Let Jesus speak to and through our hearts with brevity of words.

Action

Answer nothing when you are challenged today.

Prayer

Father God, give us the desire of our hearts—to keep silent when it's called for. Words not said don't have to be forgiven. We want to follow Your Son's example. Amen.

Reflection

Have Stability

Wisdom and knowledge will be the stability of your times, and the strength of salvation; the fear of the LORD is His treasure.
—ISAIAH 33:6

Scripture Reading: Isaiah 33:1-12

Stability means: "the strength to stand or endure; firmness; the property of a body that causes it, when disturbed from a condition of equilibrium, to develop forces that restore the original condition."

Today's verse gives quite a promise! When we feel shaken, God is firm and stands and endures for us. He will always restore us to a condition of stability, no matter what.

Change is a factor in all our lives—if not today, then surely tomorrow or the next day. Isn't it wonderful to know that when it comes, we can go to God's Word to find strength to see us through another situation? Let's not wait for the storm before we seek verses that comfort and direct. It's better to be prepared when those days appear on the horizon by having these fantastic truths in our memory banks. Nothing surpasses the comfort of knowing the truths that confirm His faithfulness to us and having the knowledge that He is our stability.

Action
Memorize Isaiah 33:6.

Prayer
Father God, prepare in our hearts those Scriptures that will give us everlasting stability in our lives. Amen.

Reflection

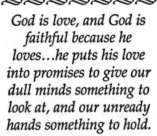

God is love, and God is faithful because he loves...he puts his love into promises to give our dull minds something to look at, and our unready hands something to hold.

—ALEXANDER RALEIGH

Select Your Friends Wisely

But I have called you friends.
—JOHN 15:15

Scripture Reading: John 15:9-17

There are those who pass like ships in the night who meet for a moment, then sail out of sight with never a backwards glance of regret; folks we know briefly then quickly forget. Then there are friends who sail together through quiet waters and stormy weather helping each other through joy and through strife. And they are the kind who give meaning to life.

—SOURCE UNKNOWN

As parents we often counsel our children to be very careful who they choose for friends, and we give the same counsel to young married couples. We are characterized by who our friends are. We suggest you interview friends as you would a future employee. Get to know them, go out to lunch, or dinner, or a picnic. See where their values are, what they believe in, what their dreams are.

Friends have a positive or negative effect upon our lives. There are certain situations when we can't choose who we are around, such as work, church, neighbors, and social clubs. Often in these settings we are thrown together. However, in our family and private times, we can be very discriminating. Our time and energy are among our most precious assets; therefore, it's important to make wise choices in our selection of people we will spend time with. Are they people who build us up and encourage us to be better people? Are they people we can respect and trust? Do we have something to offer them—to uplift and inspire them?

Action

Friends can turn everyday occasions into celebrations just by their presence. Celebrate with them today.

Prayer

Father God, open our eyes so that we won't be blinded when we look for good friends. Lead us to those who will be builders of our faith. Amen.

Reflection

Do You Blend In or Stand Out?

*Whoever desires to come after Me, let him deny himself,
and take up his cross, and follow Me.*

—MARK 8:34

Scripture Reading: Mark 8:34-38

We are amazed when we meet individuals who don't look or act like Christians, but in conversation they share that they attended church when they were younger and accepted Jesus as their personal Savior. Their present lives certainly don't reflect those early childhood decisions, yet they still classify themselves as Christians.

Charles Spurgeon once stated, "What would her Majesty think of her soldiers if they would swear they were loyal and true, yet were to say, 'Your Majesty, we prefer not to wear these uniforms; let us wear the dress of civilians! We are right honest men and upright, but do not care to stand in your ranks; we had rather slink into the enemy's camp and not wear anything that would mark us as being your soldiers!'" Spurgeon went on to comment, "Some of you do the same with Christ. You are going to be secret Christians and slink into the devil's camp and into Christ's camp, but acknowledged by neither."

A true Christian is neither ashamed of the gospel nor a shame to the gospel. George Duffield, Jr., in his famous hymn, based on a sermon by Dudley Tyng, boldly wrote:

> Stand up, stand up for Jesus
> Ye soldiers of the cross!
> Lift high His royal banner—
> It must not suffer loss.

Action

Be determined to stand up for Jesus. Don't straddle the fence.

Prayer

Father God, as a couple we want to stand up and be counted as authentic Christians. Amen.

Reflection

Burning Our Candles

But at midnight Paul and Silas were praying and singing hymns to God, and the prisoners were listening to them.

—ACTS 16:25

Scripture Reading: Acts 16:25-34

---

*I*n today's hectic schedule, we all find ourselves under great pressure to perform. We have lost sight of the fact that it is more important "to be" rather than "to do." Life is filled with pressure to be, pressure to do, pressure to perform, and pressure to produce. How can we release the pressures from the accelerated pace of our earthly lives?

In today's Scripture reading, Paul and Silas are in prison waiting to be tried, convicted, and executed for teaching the gospel. What pressure! What did they do? They were praying and singing hymns—being witnesses to the prisoners listening to them. What a revelation for us today: Slow down and sing a song of praise. When we do, we'll find that our priorities have changed. We will be more relaxed within our minds, our souls, and our spirits. Remember: Say no to good things and save your yes for the best.

Action

Take time today to pray and sing a song of praise.

Prayer

Father God, let us blow out one end of the candle and concentrate on the flame at the other end. Your light will lighten our paths. Amen.

Reflection

≈≈≈≈≈≈≈≈

Those who call to mind the sufferings of Christ and who offer up their own to God through His passion find their pains sweet and pleasant.

—St. Mary Magdalene de Pazzi

≈≈≈≈≈≈≈≈

Live for Today

Whereas you do not know what will happen tomorrow...
—JAMES 4:14

Scripture Reading: James 4:13-17

In April 1995, the tragic bombing of a federal building in Oklahoma City surprised and shocked our nation. The great mass of injury and death of the old and the young horrified us. As a nation we couldn't believe that another human being could deliberately bring such devastation to other people. Not only were those who were killed and injured touched by tragedy, but many others in their families and communities were also deeply affected. Responding to the nation's loss, the president of the United States promised swift justice to those who committed this terrible crime.

Once while we were in Oklahoma City doing a seminar, our hostess drove us by this area. The remains of the building had been razed, and the lot was going to become a park to commemorate what had occurred there on that eventful spring day. There were countless people milling around the fenced off area and gazing into space. Many carried flowers to lean against the fence. Others had hand-made cards to leave at the site. There was no smiling or laughter. The scene was very sober with tears streaming down the faces of many of the mourners.

It was a very solemn occasion, and one we will never forget. We were struck with the notion that life can end suddenly, even while we are doing ordinary activities such as being at our desk at work, standing next to a copy machine, or sending a fax.

We all expect tomorrow to come and assume we will be able to fulfill all of our plans. Tomorrow I'll get my life in order; tomorrow I'll spend more time with my family; tomorrow I'll be a better husband (a better wife); tomorrow I'll go to church; tomorrow I'll tell my family I love them!

But only God knows if there will be a tomorrow for us. Since we don't know about tomorrow, we had better start today what we planned for tomorrow—tomorrow may never come.

Action

Do today what you've been putting off. Don't wait for tomorrow.

Prayer

Father God, today we will love, say edifying words to our family, be encouragements to those around us, hug our children—all those things that we were going to do tomorrow. Amen.

Reflection

The Two Shall Become One

So we, being many, are one body in Christ, and individually members of one another.

—ROMANS 12:5

Scripture Reading: Romans 12:3-8

It seems as though "unity and oneness" are so very difficult for the "me" people to understand and apply to their daily walk. People state, "I have my bank account and my mate has his (or hers)." "This is my car." "These are my children." "I want to take my vacation alone." As a society, many of us have learned not to trust anyone other than ourselves. Teamwork is a virtue taught at an early age, but when left on our own, we revert back to our sinful, selfish nature. Ask any coach and they will tell you teamwork is very difficult to teach. Everyone wants to be the star.

In Scripture we often hear the terms "one spirit," "one belief," "one life," and "one another." That's when we begin to realize that God wants us to grow in oneness. Togetherness helps bind our relationship with God. Early in the book of Genesis we read, "Therefore a man shall leave his father and mother and be joined to his wife, and they shall become one flesh" (2:24).

When we join forces with others we become stronger. This concept is at the center of why we need to be in a church that's teaching God's Word. We need the support of others if we are to grow spiritually in our walks. Here are some Scriptures that impress upon us the importance of oneness:

1 Corinthians
    1:10 — Agree with one another
    10:24 — Look out for one another
    16:20 — Greet one another with a holy kiss

Galatians
    5:13 — Serve one another
    6:1 — Carry one another's burdens

Ephesians
    4:2 — Bear with one another
    4:32 — Be kind to one another
    5:19 — Speak to one another with psalms, hymns, and spiritual songs
    5:21 — Submit to one another

Action

Check out your speech and see how often you use me, me, me, or us, us, us. Evaluate your oneness, and make changes where needed.

Prayer

Father God, if we aren't reflecting oneness in our family life, give us the necessary conviction so we will bend in the proper direction. Give us strength and courage to make these changes. Amen.

Reflection

Be Strong in Weakness

When I am weak, then I am strong.
—2 CORINTHIANS 12:10

Scripture Reading: 2 Corinthians 12:7-10

As we travel around southern California, it is obvious that we live in an area that stresses good health practices. We see joggers, bikers, surfers, and beach sports. Weightlifting, jazzercising, and marathon races are popular, and this area is a haven for triathlons. People want to be healthy, extend their lives, and improve their strength. We all strive to enjoy the goodness of life through good health, but Scripture tells us that when we are weak, then we are strong. How can that be? It seems so contrary to our thoughts.

Throughout our walk through life, we know that we grow the most when we are weak. It is during these precious moments that we are more apt to talk with God and cast all our excuses away. During these times we stop looking at life through rose-colored glasses. We see life as it really is. We will never be so near to God as during trials and our lives will be changed forever. When weakened by circumstances, don't shy away. Go forth knowing that you are growing in Christ.

Action

Know that in your weakness you are strong.

Prayer

Father God, from real life we know that we become stronger when we are weak. Thank You for this principle. Amen.

Reflection

~~~~~~~

God promises to make the vale of trouble a door of hope.

—JILL BRISCOE

~~~~~~~

We Choose the Color

Yet I will rejoice in the LORD, I will joy in the God of my salvation.

—HABAKKUK 3:18

Scripture Reading: Habakkuk 3

Even when we face disaster, illness, death, bankruptcy, or other ills of life we can rejoice. An elderly woman who was down on her luck had a friend who stated, "Sorrow does color life, doesn't it?" "Yes," the woman agreed, then added, "but I will choose the colors."

We know from personal experience that we can choose the colors by how we respond to difficulties. Making the decision to remain positive isn't a denial of pain; it's a willful act of trust based on the truth that God will remain with us to be our strength, shield, healer, and protector. We daily choose to rejoice or not to rejoice. We consent to be a victim or a victor.

Action

How are you painting your life today? What will you do today to rejoice in your situation?

Prayer

> Father God, we needed to be reminded that we can choose to rejoice. Thank You for giving us a palette with variety. We want to be known as people with many colors. Amen.

Reflection

Oh Lord my God, I thank thee that Thou has brought this day to a close; I thank Thee that Thou hast given me peace in body and in soul. Thy hand has been over me and has protected and preserved me.

—DIETRICH BONHOEFFER

What Do We See and Hear?

All things are lawful for me, but I will not be brought under the power of any.
—1 CORINTHIANS 6:12

Scripture Reading: 1 Corinthians 6:12-20

Ted Koppel, the news anchor for ABC's "Nightline," stated in a recent commencement address: "We have constructed the Tower of Babel, and it is a television antenna." No greater influence impacts our thinking than the media in all its forms. Since our media is primarily controlled by secular humanists, the slant of most print copy, programming, advertising, and news portrays a secular worldview. For instance, the life portrayed on TV loves pleasure and sensuality, doesn't deny itself anything, and has a right to whatever goal it sets.

Perhaps the only way to overcome this dilemma is to reevaluate our sources of entertainment and information. Our concern is that our minds will be influenced in an area in which it's difficult to be on guard against or resist.

The insidious power of television is destroying family life. As parents, we have to take control of what we allow to come into our homes. Try not turning on your TV for one week and see how your family responds. This will help you evaluate the influence TV has on your family. When TV does come on, be very selective in what you watch.

Action

Make a list of what you can do to build up your family when so much of society is trying to tear it down.

Prayer

Father God, make us aware of those things that steal from us. Give us the courage to be strong. Amen.

Reflection

Be Doers of the Word

Be doers of the word, and not hearers only,
deceiving yourselves.

—JAMES 1:22

Scripture Reading: James 1:21-27

Religion is usually caught and rarely taught. Andrew Carnegie once said, "The longer I live, the less I listen to what men say and the more I watch what they do." Action is always superior to speech in the four Gospels. That is why the Word became flesh and not newsprint. The oft-quoted words of Edgar Guest offer profound truth:

> I would rather see a sermon than hear one anyday;
> I would rather one would walk with me than merely show the way;
> The eye's a better student and more willing than the ear,
> Fine counsel is confusing, but example's always clear,
> And the best of all the teachers are the ones who live their creeds,
> For to see good put into action is what everybody needs.
> I soon can learn to do it if you'll let me see it done;

I can watch your hands in action, but your tongue
too fast may run.
The lectures you deliver may be wise and true,
But I'd rather get my lessons by observing what you
do;
For I might misunderstand you and the high advice
you give.
But there's no misunderstanding how you act and
how you live.[8]

Action

We encourage the two of you not to say a word
about your faith today. Instead—show it.

Prayer

*Father God, we pray that those around us will see us
as doers of our faith instead of hearing our "clanging
cymbals." Amen.*

Reflection

What Do You See?

I know your works, that you are neither cold nor hot.
I could wish you were cold or hot.
—REVELATION 3:15

Scripture Reading: Revelation 3:14-22

Coming to a small Oklahoma town to be pastor of his first church, W.B. Alexander was met by one of his parishioners who stated flatly that the church was dead, everyone knew it, and he was surprised that such an energetic young man should begin his ministry in such a hopeless situation.

Alexander's enthusiasm was not easily defused by difficult circumstances, but he did come to see that there was a large measure of truth in the parishioner's assessment. So, in desperation, he placed a notice in the local paper announcing that because everyone agreed that the church was dead, the funeral would be held the next Sunday afternoon. When the time came, the church was crowded with the curious, who were rewarded by the sight of a large coffin banked with flowers at the front of the sanctuary. Alexander preached a brief sermon and. then invited the people to pay their last respects.

As the long queue passed by, each one looked into the coffin, then glanced guiltily away. In the bottom of the coffin lay a mirror, solemnly reflecting the last remains of the church—the startled faces of the congregation.[9]

Whether this story is fact or fiction, there is truth in it. The vitality of any church is in direct proportion to the "aliveness" of those who comprise its membership. Friedrich Nietzsche once said to a group of Christian men, "You are going to have to look more redeemed if I am to believe in your Redeemer."

Action

As you go out in today's world, make it a point to look and act redeemed.

Prayer

Father God, as we look into the mirror we want to see two excited Christians whereby the world knows that we are joyful about our faith. Amen.

Reflection

The Source of Wisdom

The fear of the LORD is the beginning of knowledge,
but fools despise wisdom and instruction.
—PROVERBS 1:7

Scripture Reading: Proverbs 1:1-7

A man will learn to discipline himself or someone else will." Isn't that the truth! We will discipline ourselves or someone else will—maybe a teacher, a coach, a juvenile officer, a judge, a prison warden, a drill sergeant, a parent, society, or God. Someone will teach you. If you don't learn, you will fail in life.

In the book of Proverbs, Solomon offers advice on how we should conduct ourselves in various situations in everyday life. His basic instruction is to fear and trust the Lord. Solomon challenges us to continually seek God's wisdom for the decisions we make. Remember: What happens tomorrow depends on the decisions we make today.

Personal discipline goes beyond academic accomplishments to moral responsibility. It focuses on decision-making and shows itself best in our self-control and moral living.

Action

Adopt a wisdom verse that the two of you can use in living your life together. Write it down and memorize it.

Prayer

Father God, show us Your ways that we might acknowledge You as God. Help us know Your ways. Amen.

Reflection

~~~~~~~~

He who reigns within himself and rules his passions, desires, and fears is more than a king.

—MILTON

~~~~~~~~

The Power of the Word

The message of the cross is foolishness to those who are perishing, but to us who are being saved it is the power of God.

—1 CORINTHIANS 1:18

Scripture Reading: 1 Corinthians 1:17-29

All around us are people who believe that Scripture is foolish. They think that people who depend on God and His Word need a crutch to get through life. However, Paul calls the message of the cross "the power of God"—and Scripture presents that message. Power comes from the Greek word *dunamis*, which our word *dynamite* comes from. Anyone who considers God's Word to be useless will eventually experience the full impact of God. The power of God's Word, when it explodes, leads to a life of freedom.

There's a Chinese tale about a young man who captured a tiger cub, brought it home, and raised it in a cage. When it was full grown, the man bragged about how ferocious and powerful it was. "That tiger isn't wild anymore," scoffed his friends. "He's as tame as an old house cat." This went on until a wise old man overheard them and said, "There's only one way to know whether this tiger is ferocious or not. Open the cage!" The young man smiled, placed his hand on the latch, and challenged his friends, "Want to try out my tiger?"

Even though Scripture may sometimes seem tame and foolish, don't be surprised at its power when it is released into your life.

Action

Understand that God's Word is powerful and destroys the chains of sin.

Prayer

Father God, we have experienced Your power. We thank You for breaking the chain of original sin. Amen.

Reflection

~~~~~~~~~

No man or woman can really be strong, gentle, pure, and good without the world being better for it.

—PHILLIP BROOKS

~~~~~~~~~

Like the Wings of Eagles

But those who wait on the LORD shall renew their strength;
they shall mount up with wings like eagles, they shall run and
not be weary, they shall walk and not faint.
—ISAIAH 40:31

Scripture Reading: Isaiah 40:27-31

We love to watch the Discovery channel on television because it is so educational and informative on many topics. One such episode was the study of the majestic bald eagle. They have beautiful flying patterns, and their wings are powerful as they stretch out to catch the wind currents near the cliffs where they live.

Scripture also uses the eagle to picture strength. Those who wait or depend on the Lord will exchange their weaknesses for God's strength. Neither soaring with wings as eagles nor running is presented as the end goal. Rather, the main thought is that "walking" is the mainstay of the Christian experience. The most exciting times don't take place when we soar, but it's how we get through the monotonous and everyday grind of life that illustrates God's power.

Eagles go through a time in life when they become very weak and defenseless. They retire to a hiding place in a cave out of reach of predators and experience a period of renewal. With their great beaks, they pull out their mighty wing feathers one by one, then they extract each claw. Finally, they begin to smash their beaks against the rocks until it, too, is gone. Left defenseless, these peerless, unique birds wait patiently until beak, talons, and feathers have regrown. They emerge in renewed condition stronger than ever before.

Action

> Are you in a situation where you need to walk rather than soar? Be willing to wait on the Lord.

Prayer

> *Father God, we certainly want to wait upon You. Help us to be satisfied when we are only able to walk. Amen.*

Reflection

Be Kind

*Be kind to one another, tenderhearted, forgiving one another,
just as God in Christ forgave you.*
—EPHESIANS 4:32

Scripture Reading: Ephesians 4:25-32

One of the best compliments we can give our friends is to tell them they are kind people. And we spend a lot of time teaching our children to be kind not only to people but also to animals. When we look at the biblical concept of kindness, we see that this virtue is "a gentle or tender action that comes from a spirit of concern or compassion." All through Scripture God's character is revealed as we discover His many attributes of kindness. A kind person goes out of his or her way to be nice to someone else. A tender heart is reflected by caring for others, being mindful of their needs. Thoughtfulness and graciousness are very much attitudes of the heart.

Each day we can lighten someone's load and bring him or her joy by being considerate. It is worth it to make others feel important and cared for. Say "good morning" and ask, "How are you?" Volunteer—"Let me help you with that load" or "I'd like to get that door for you." Even a bright smile paired with a genuine compliment conveys kindness. Heartfelt words and helpful deeds will always ease another person's day. Who among us would not like to have our load decreased even for a short time?

Action
Be a blessing in someone's life today.

Prayer
Father God, thank You for modeling for us how to be kind. May we pass Your abundant love to others. Amen.

Reflection

~~~~~~~~
*If I can right a human
wrong,
If I can help to make
one strong,
If I can cheer with smile,
or song,
Lord show me how.*
—GRENVILLE KLEISER
~~~~~~~~

Yielding

Incline your hearts to the LORD God of Israel.
—JOSHUA 24:23

Scripture Reading: Joshua 24:19-24

As we drive the busy southern California freeways and streets, we often wonder how many people would lose their lives if they hadn't learned to yield to let someone go ahead of them, or if they hadn't learned to yield when the street sign reads "yield to oncoming traffic." Yielding is so important because, by being courteous, drivers can actually prevent harm from coming to them.

Relaxing our need to be in control also has very many benefits.

A second-grade teacher was holding the hand of one of her learning-disabled students. The teacher began to trace in the air the pattern of the letter "A," which she was trying to teach this young boy. His muscles were tense, resisting the teacher's guidance. She moved his arm through the air in a large pattern. Over and over they spoke the letter name and sound as they wrote the letter in the air. Slowly the boy's arm muscles relaxed and caught the pattern. They soon became one in sound and motion. When the teacher felt confident in what the student had learned, she requested that he take a piece of chalk and approach the blackboard. With great assurance the boy printed out the large letter "A" that he had practiced in the air with his teacher. The teacher loudly applauded as both their faces broke out with wide smiles and gleams in their eyes.

The teacher's desire for that young student was to guide him, but only as he gave up control to the teacher could he learn the pattern of the letter.

God's desire is also to guide us, but only as we yield are we able to learn the pattern of living that God longs for us to grasp. Sometimes it is so difficult to "let go and let God," but peace and happiness come when we do. When striving ceases, worries fall away.

Action

Trust God that He will guide you into righteousness. Yield to Him today!

Prayer

Father God, as our teacher and as our God, we want to yield to Your training. Help us learn how to relax when we feel tense. Amen.

Reflection

Approaching God's Throne

Holy, holy, holy is the LORD of hosts;
the whole earth is full of His glory!
—ISAIAH 6:3

Scripture Reading: Isaiah 6:1-9

---

*G*od is not one among many; He is the *one and only*. The word *holy* means "unique, set apart, unlike all others." When holy is repeated three times, that expresses the superlative degree. This emphasis stresses God's righteousness in contrast to our sinfulness.

Holiness is who God is—not what God does. All of God's attributes flow out of His holiness. That is why He is not capable of the slightest hint of impurity, unrighteousness, untruth, injustice, or misuse of power. How do we approach this holy God? Before we go to prayer, we need to pause and consider whom we are calling.

When Moses approached God, he was told to remove his sandals (see Exodus 3:5). This indicates that we are to stop to take off our shoes when we are on holy ground. What does this mean today, and what are other considerations for approaching God?

- Approach His glory with boldness (John 17:24).

181

- Recognize that our Father is in heaven (Matthew 6:9).

- Praise God (Luke 19:37; Revelation 19:5).

- Rejoice in Jesus our Savior (Luke 1:46,47).

- All in God's temple cry out "Glory!" (Psalm 29:9).

- Offer thanksgiving without ceasing (1 Thessalonians 5:16,17; Romans 11:36).

- Give glory to God (John 17:22).

If we take time to prepare our hearts for prayer, our spirits are more in tune with God's Spirit. When we get a glimpse of God's glory, we gain something of it for ourselves. When we secure His glory, then God may be glorified in us. "Blessed are the pure in heart, for they shall see God" (Matthew 5:8).

Prayer is not a burden or a duty to fulfill. It is unlimited joy and power. The gift of prayer was given so that we may "find grace to help in time of need" (Hebrews 4:16).

Action

Prepare your hearts before you go to God with your petitions.

Prayer

Father God, we want to have powerful prayer lives. We want to meet You face to face. When we pray, we want to see Your glory. Amen.

Reflection

Give Me a New Song

Oh, sing to the LORD a new song!
Sing to the LORD, all the earth.
Sing to the LORD, bless His name; proclaim the good news
of His salvation from day to day.
—PSALM 96:1,2

Scripture Reading: Psalm 33:1-22

Does reading yesterday's newspaper or hearing a day-old event on television or radio excite you? Not us! We like to keep current with what's happening. Everybody at the office wants to talk about current events—not the old stuff.

That same need to remain fresh and up-to-date applies to our recognition of the good things God does for us. We must consider His mercies to be "new every morning." In today's verse, the psalm writer calls out for a new song. He desires a new appreciation of what the Lord has done for us in the past as well as what He is doing now.

Embrace the fresh perspective of Psalm 33 because God is still doing great things today. Look around and see the manifestations of God's handiwork. See how today's new song is revealed in nature and in humanity. Then praise the God behind it!

Action

Step out with a new song. Note one new thing you have observed of God's creation. Report back to your spouse tonight at dinner.

Prayer

Father God, You are truly awesome. Give us a new song each day. Let us become alert to the glory of You in the life around us. Amen.

Reflection

What Makes a Church Alive?

*For by grace you have been saved through faith,
and that not of yourselves; it is the gift of God,
not of works, lest any one should boast.*
—EPHESIANS 2:8,9

Scripture Reading: Ephesians 2:1-10

America is on the move. Gone are the days when families lived in the same community all their lives. Now, staying in one place for four or five years is fortunate. In an upwardly mobile society, we are on the move for many reasons. One of the consequences of moving is that we are constantly relocating our church life. Some people stop going altogether, some take a vacation from responsibilities, and some spend a great deal of time searching out a new church. There is so much to take into consideration, such as: denomination, depth of teaching, youth groups, support groups, cross-section of ages, and mission out-reach.

What makes a church alive? It is not soft seats and subdued lights. It's a strong, courageous laity and devoted leaders who deal with controversial issues in society in biblical ways. It is not the pleasing tones of the organ, but pleasant people who, though gentle, are firm in their convictions and resolute in their actions. It is not tall towers and chiming bells, but the lofty vision of the church's people and the clear ring of the affirmation of their faith. It is the layperson who remembers to keep Sundays—and weekdays—holy with acts of love and kindness.

The late Cardinal Cushing said:

> If all the sleeping folks will wake up, and all the lukewarm folks will fire up, and all the dishonest folks will confess up, and all the disgruntled folks will sweeten up, and all the discouraged folks will cheer up, and all the depressed folks will look up, and all the estranged folks will make up, and all the gossipers will shut up, and all the true church members will pray up, and the savior for all is lifted up, then you can have the world's greatest renewal, and the church will be fully alive and well."[10]

Action

Evaluate your church to see if it's alive. If not, consider finding a church that is alive—or helping your church revive.

Prayer

Father God, we thank You for directing us to a church that teaches the gospel in New Testament fashion. Amen.

Reflection

Be a Light to the World

Do all things without complaining and disputing, that you may become blameless and harmless, children of God without fault in the midst of a crooked and perverse generation, among whom you shine as lights in the world.
—PHILIPPIANS 2:14,15

Scripture Reading: Philippians 2:12-16

Have you ever become discouraged at home or work because you felt you were the only Christian around? Have you had days when it seemed that nobody cared about goodness and they laughed and made fun of you because of your faith? One person had the same dilemma about her workplace, and she wanted to quit work until her pastor asked this very penetrating question: "Where do people usually put lights?" "In dark places," the lady replied. And she quickly recognized that her place of work was indeed a dark place that needed to have light. She stayed at her job.

As "lights in the world," believers in Christ have the privilege of illuminating dark places. If you are in an unusually difficult and ungodly atmosphere, remember Christ's words: "Let your light so shine before men, that

187

they may see your good works and glorify your Father in heaven" (Matthew 5:16). Light is always needed where there is darkness.

Action

> Go out into the darkness and light up someone's life.

Prayer

> *Father God, help us be lights in a dark world. Let our lights dispel darkness. Amen.*

Reflection

It's Who You Know That Counts

But God is the Judge: He puts down one, and exalts another.
—PSALM 75:7

Scripture Reading: Psalm 75:1-10

We're sure you have heard the expression, "It's who you know that counts." Depending upon your experiences in life, you might say, "Right on; so true." Other people may shout, "That's not fair!" because this principle seems contrary to fair play and competition. "It's who you know" doesn't give people of equal abilities an equal opportunity for success.

Being known by the right person does shorten some of the processes of life. Having a relationship with your banker speeds up the loan process. Always using the same pharmacist may mean you won't have to stand in line. Supporting your pastor may make planning easier with your wedding. Being acquainted with your mechanic may save you money on car repairs. Knowing the right person *can* make life easier.

In Psalm 75, we read that the Lord "puts down one, and exalts another." This means that the almighty God is behind the scenes giving His own kind of breaks, opportunities, and promotions—all according to His mercy and grace. Because we know Him, we are privileged to many opportunities that nonbelievers don't have.

The resources of God are at our disposal, as well as His unlimited power to work for our good through all circumstances. Being in relationship with God through our Lord Jesus Christ does matter!

Action

Take advantage of knowing God. Accept His blessings.

Prayer

Father God, we are thankful that we know You and that Your power is our power. We are glad that You love us. Amen.

Reflection

Look to the One

They let down the bed on which the paralytic was lying.
—MARK 2:4

Scripture Reading: Mark 2:1-12

Everywhere we go in southern California there are crowds. People, people, people. Even freeways are packed with cars filled with people. If we go to Disneyland, Knott's Berry Farm, or Sea World, we have to stand in long lines. In today's world of handouts, welfare, people on street corners asking for money, it's difficult to discern who is truly in need. Yet we're called to reach out to others—even when it's uncomfortable or inconvenient.

Jesus was never too busy to help any individual in need. One day when our Savior was preaching in a house at Capernaum, the crowd was so large that it was standing room only. Yet four men who had a very sick friend realized they must get him to Jesus without delay. After carrying him to the roof, they made an opening and lowered the bed on which the crippled man lay. This was very disturbing to those in attendance, but Jesus, sensing the four men's faith and the man's need, healed his body and forgave his sins. Christ always had time for someone who needed help.

Action

Pick out someone in the crowd who has a need, and minister to him or her.

Prayer

Father God, help us look into the masses and select someone who needs to be touched with Your love. Enable us to meet the needs of that person. Amen.

Reflection

~~~~~~

Life is an exciting business and most exciting when it is lived for others.

—HELEN KELLER

~~~~~~

Lift Up Your Soul

To You, O LORD, I lift up my soul.
—PSALM 25:1

Scripture Reading: Psalm 25:1-5

Prayer can seem such a mystery. When do we pray, how do we pray, what do we say, what language do we speak, what body posture do we use? And what exactly is prayer? One answer is that prayer is asking things from God, but surely we know prayer is more than that.

Biblical dictionaries define prayer as "a wish directed toward God." When we pray, we are talking to God. It is really lifting our souls to God. When we do this, God has an opportunity to do what He will do in us and with us. We make ourselves available to Him. An old Jewish saying puts it wonderfully: "Prayer is the moment when heaven and earth kiss each other." Prayer certainly is not our attempt to persuade God to do our will; however, it may release His power.

Some people think prayer is only for emergencies. Danger threatens, sicknesses come, things are lacking, difficulties arise—then they pray like the atheist in a coal mine...when the roof began to fall, he began to pray.

Prayer reminds us that we are utterly dependent upon God. We draw closer to God and become more knowledgeable about Him when we talk to Him. The more we discover about God, the richer our lives become.

Action

Praise God today for allowing you direct access to Him through prayer.

Prayer

Father God, we feel so inadequate when we pray. We ask for Your guidance—teach us how to pray. We want to know more of You! Amen.

Reflection

Life Is a Gift

*For we brought nothing into this world, and it is
certain we can carry nothing out.*

—1 TIMOTHY 6:7

Scripture Reading: 1 Timothy 6:3-10

We all search for contentment. During our recent bout with cancer and not knowing from one blood test to the other if that terminal "big C" would reappear, we have looked at life in a very different way than when we were both healthy. One of the secrets of contentment is to realize that life is a gift, not a right.

It is only when we recognize life as temporary that we truly come to grips with what is important. When we face our own mortality, our priorities quickly come into focus. We find real meaning in our lives when we consider life as a gift from God. Every moment is precious, so we must cherish each one.

Don't wait until you have to come to grips with the awareness that you only have a short time to love, care, laugh, cry, write letters, make phone calls, or enjoy your friends. It might be too late! Do it now while there is time.

Action
  Realize that life is a precious gift to enjoy today.

Prayer
  Father God, how precious life is. Let us not take it for granted. May we get caught up on all that we have put off until tomorrow. Amen.

Reflection

~~~~~~~~

Let those live now, who never lov'd before; let those who always lov'd now love the more.

—LATIN PROVERB

~~~~~~~~

ℬe Content

I have learned in whatever state I am, to be content.
—PHILIPPIANS 4:11

Scripture Reading: Philippians 4:8-13

O Lord, give me the grace to be
Content with what You give to me!
No! More than that, let me rejoice
In all You send me—it's your choice!

—AUTHOR UNKNOWN

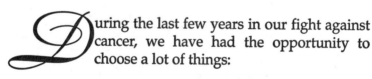uring the last few years in our fight against cancer, we have had the opportunity to choose a lot of things:

- What specialist we would put our confidence in
- What hospital we would go to for treatment
- Whether we would go along with our doctors' recommendations
- If we would accept experimental procedures
- If we would blame God
- If we would deny our faith in an almighty God
- Whether we would continue to smile
- Whether we would continue a strong prayer life

We have found that we may not be able to choose our circumstances, but we can certainly choose how we are going to relate to them. Whatever happens, we choose to draw on the power of the Holy Spirit for the strength and courage we need.

Action

What decisions are the two of you facing today? Write them down, then discuss how you are going to respond to them.

Prayer

Father God, we can do all things through Christ who strengthens us. Give us peace about our choices. We put them before You so You can know our every request. Give us contentment. Amen.

Reflection

Do Good unto Others

Every good gift and every perfect gift is from above.
—James 1:17

Scripture Reading: James 1:12-18

---

*D*id you know that the Greek word for "good" appears more than 100 times in the New Testament? The translations of the word vary, and include such meanings as genuine, honorable, healthy, generous, dependable, and honest. Goodness involves habitual actions that reflect a person's inward disposition. (This includes the concept of helping but, interestingly enough, can also include rebuking, correcting, and discipline.) Long before the present-day teaching about "excellence" in business, education, or church work, Paul taught this virtuous concept to the early church.

As maturing Christians, we are to grow into people of goodness. Each day we have the opportunity to show this fruit at work in our lives. The first step is to become aware of those around us who need a touch of kindness. Much as we'd like to, we can't show love to the whole world. We certainly can touch those with whom we have daily contact—spouses, children, extended families, neighbors, and coworkers.

The world is hungry for goodness. Goodness is love in action. We live in a society longing for people who will give of themselves to enrich the lives of others.

Action

Proclaim God's wonderful nature by being good.

Prayer

Father God, may the goodness we show others be a reflection of how much we love You. Help us show Your love to a hurting world. Amen.

Reflection

~~~~~~~~
If you don't stand for something, you'll fall for anything.

—UNKNOWN
~~~~~~~~

In the End, What?

Well done, good and faithful servant; you were faithful over a few things, I will make you ruler over many things.
—MATTHEW 25:21

Scripture Reading: Matthew 25:14-30

Emilie's Uncle Al was a young man when he and his parents landed in New York City from Romania. Knowing very little English, having very little money, and without a job, he was lonely and, except for a willingness to learn, he lacked the tools to start out life in this new country called America. He worked in whatever job was available, saved his money, and continued westward to California. He started to work in the back office of a shoe company doing whatever was requested by his boss. Since he was focused and dedicated to this entry-level job, he rapidly worked his way up. He became the president of the Innes Shoe Company. He went from a flat in New York to a beautiful home in BelAir, one of the most prestigious residential areas in Los Angeles. Al is a great example of someone who received the blessings that go along with today's verse.

As we stand before God someday, we want to be known as people who were faithful with the little things in life. We want to hear God say, "Well done, good and faithful servant." Do you? Are you just starting, or still experiencing, the little things regarding your life and career? Are you getting anxious for more? Be patient, stay focused, and go the extra mile. Keep looking to God, and little by little you will be given more and more responsibility.

Action
>   Volunteer for something you have never done before. Stretch yourself.

Prayer
>   Father God, we want to be known as good and faithful servants. Assist us in our goal. Amen.

Reflection

Give Me the Easy Life

*A little sleep, a little slumber, a little folding
of the hands to sleep.*

—PROVERBS 6:10

Scripture Reading: Proverbs 6:6-11

I want it now! I don't want to work hard to get it, either. Please give me pleasure. I want the easy life.

The "sluggard" is mentioned a number of times in Proverbs. His procrastination and lack of initiative are strongly condemned. His foolishness is evident in his lack of preparation for the future; rather, he prefers to stay in bed (Proverbs 6:9-10). As he waits and does nothing, opportunities slip away. Without notice, poverty and need will overwhelm him.

God expects us to work. In fact, one of the very first work assignments God gave to Adam and Eve was to take care of the Garden of Eden. There are no easy jobs in life. Those who refuse to be industrious will eventually be rudely awakened from their daydreams, for desperate need and grinding poverty are sure to come (see Proverbs 24:30-34).

The master was a worker
With daily work to do,
And if you would be like Him
you must be zealous too.
—AUTHOR UNKNOWN

Action

Be zealous in your work. Thank God for giving you the vision to prepare yourself for excellence.

Prayer

Father God, we are not looking for the easy life. In all that we do we want to give honor to Your name. Amen.

Reflection

The Golden Years

And even to gray hairs I will carry you! I have made, and I will bear; even I will carry, and will deliver you.

—ISAIAH 46:4

Scripture Reading: Isaiah 46:1-4

As we look at what the media throws before us, we may think the only important people in our society are the youth. Everywhere we look we see advertisements and movies featuring younger folks. It used to be that over 60 was old, but now it seems like over 40 is old. We're taught to cling to outward beauty (cosmetic surgery is at an all-time high), youthful strength (workout centers are open 24 hours a day), and vocational achievement because staying young is the key to contentment.

The Scriptures offer us repeated assurances that the aging process is completely secure in God's hands. God has a unique plan for each of us—regardless of our ages! His schedule will carry us through the changing seasons of life. When we realize this, we can be at peace with the aging process. Each day of life that God gives is ordained according to His perfect wisdom.

Those who live each day for Christ will bear fruit not only in youth but also in old age. The psalmist writes that "those who are planted in the house of the LORD shall flourish...[and] shall still bear fruit in old age; they shall be fresh and flourishing" (Psalm 92:13,14).

Action
Step out in faith that God has a plan for your life.

Prayer
Father God, no matter what our ages, we want to be used by You daily. Amen.

Reflection

~~~~~~~~~~~~~~
*Find joy in simplicity, self-respect,
and indifference to what lies
between virtue and vice. Love the
human race. Follow the divine.*
—MARCUS AURELIUS
~~~~~~~~~~~~~~

Let Your Heavenly Father Help

Offer the sacrifices of righteousness, and put your trust in the LORD.

—PSALM 4:5

Scripture Reading: Psalm 4

How many times do we struggle with our everyday situations? As independent people, we tend to try to solve all of our problems by ourselves. Today's reading says we are to put our trust in the Lord.

British evangelist Billy Strachan tells of a time when he was sitting in his study, engaged in a serious discussion with a friend. His daughter walked into the room holding her jump rope that was all tangled up. She handed it to her dad and quietly left. Continuing his intense conversation with his friend, Billy untied the knots in her rope almost without thinking. A few minutes later his daughter returned and said, "Thanks, Daddy," and skipped out to play. Why can't we be like that with our heavenly Father? Why do we work so hard in our own efforts when we can turn our problems over to Him and let Him work them out?

If you're struggling with a situation at home, work, school, church, or a relationship that needs to be turned over to Jesus for help—let go, let God!

Action

Turn one of your struggles over to God. Let Him handle it for both of you. Write down the particulars in your journal, and be sure to date the entry. Check up periodically to see how God is doing.

Prayer

Father God, let us trust You and be still. Amen.

Reflection

Praise the Lord

While I live I will praise the LORD; I will sing praises
to my God while I have my being.

—PSALM 146:2

Scripture Reading: Psalm 146:1-10

---

*T*hroughout the psalms we read how the various writers come to one of the basic principles for living a balanced Christian life: We are to "praise the Lord." When we rise past the hurts and disappointments in life, we climactically shout, "Praise the Lord!" Often in our youth and when life is going great we tend to forget all that God does for us.

During our recent struggle with Emilie's cancer, we claimed John 11:4 as our praise verse: "This sickness is not unto death, but for the glory of God, that the Son of God may be glorified through it." Wherever we go, we share God's faithfulness to us through this difficult period of our lives. Where some people might be inclined to curse God for the illness, we have decided to take the higher road.

We can't tell you how many people have approached us and shared how we have modeled for them how to praise the Lord when difficulty comes. A positive witness you give for Jesus can be how you respond when times become difficult. Praise energizes your life in Jesus!

Action

In your own way, praise the Lord.

Prayer

Father God, thank You for reminding us that we are to praise You. We don't want the lessons of life to turn us negative. Amen.

Reflection

Know What You Ask For

Now make us a king to judge us like all the nations.
—1 SAMUEL 8:5

Scripture Reading: 1 Samuel 8

*O*ftentimes when we pray we want to tell God what's best for our situation. Rather then ask, we often demand. There is a story of a mother who demanded that God heal her sick son. The child was healed, but as an adult he became a hardened criminal and ultimately was executed. The mother's heart was broken, and she wished that God had taken her child when he was so gravely ill. We need to be certain that what we want from God is His perfect plan, which is sometimes quite different than our demands.

The elders of Israel demanded of the prophet Samuel that God give them a king like all the other nations had. Since Samuel had become "old and not able to lead the 12 tribes effectively," the people become impatient and didn't want to wait for God's direction. God was offended by their demand, but He told Samuel to give them a king. God also instructed Samuel to warn the tribes that some kings levy high taxes, raise large armies, and force large numbers of the population to hard labor. And that's exactly what Saul did as their new king.

Many times our requests to God are not necessarily wrong, but we must submissively ask—not demand.

Action

Evaluate your prayer requests to make sure they are of the "asking" not the "demanding" variety.

Prayer

Father God, we come to You humbly with our praises and requests. Amen.

Reflection

Praise God Daily

Seven times a day I praise You, because of Your righteous judgments.
—PSALM 119:164

Scripture Reading: Psalm 119:161-168

We have all been around people who are down in the dumps. They complain about little things and big things. Nothing looks good, tastes good, feels good, sounds good. No matter what happens, the hole gets deeper and life is just not worth living. Suicide has even crossed their minds. They think no one will miss them, and they will certainly be happier without all the pains of life.

Our Scripture today helps us break through the barrier of despair because it charges us to praise God seven times a day. No one can remain negative for very long when they are praising God in this fashion. Get into the habit of praising God for your abundance of gifts—not just for material possessions, but also for blessings of health, family, energy, church family, your country, lay ministries, nurses, Bible teachers, coaches, policemen, a bed to sleep in, clean sheets, a comfortable pillow, Social Security, retirement, vacations, and so on. There is much to be thankful for.

Action
Begin praising God seven times today.

Prayer
Father God, turn our negatives into positives! Amen.

Reflection

~~~~~~~~
*There is a substitute for
criticism. It is called love.
Love heals, love protects,
love builds up, and more
change occurs with love
than with criticism.*

—H. NORMAN WRIGHT

~~~~~~~~

Watch Your Words

But let your "Yes" be "Yes," and your "No," "No!"
—MATTHEW 5:37

Scripture Reading: Matthew 5:33-42

---

*H*ave you ever heard of someone getting in trouble for something they haven't said? During military combat when an American soldier becomes a prisoner of war, they are instructed to give only their name, rank, and serial number when being questioned by enemy interrogators. While in medical school, surgeons are instructed to weigh the importance of each word spoken during an operation. As the anesthetic is given, anxiety may strike a patient if they hear someone say, "I'm going to shoot her now." Can you imagine what the patient would feel like if he or she overheard the chief surgeon state carelessly, "This doesn't seem like a good day for me"? Depending on how a word is said and with what inflection, it can have either a positive or negative effect on the patient.

In our families, the need is the same. Our words need to lift up, not tear down those we love. It is often wiser not to say too much during times of anger. Words said are very difficult to take back. Some spoken words continue to cause pain for many years.

Action

Be very selective in the words you say today. Make sure they give encouragement, hope, and faith to the hearer.

Prayer

Father God, remind us that our spoken words need to be brief and nurturing. Help us guard our words. Amen.

Reflection

~~~~~~

When you return a blessing for an insult, you will inherit a blessing!

—LINDA DILLON

~~~~~~

The Commandment for Happiness

Happy is the man who has his quiver full of [children];
they shall not be ashamed, but shall speak
with their enemies in the gate.

—PSALM 127:5

Scripture Reading: Psalm 127

As humans, we are continually searching for happiness. We try all kinds of products, events, possessions, and experiences to find this cup of gold. When Helen Steiner Rice first started writing poems for a large greeting card company in America, she developed her own "ten commandments" for helping her find happiness during the dark periods of her life. They were:

1. Thou shalt be happy.
2. Thou shalt use thy talents to make others glad.
3. Thou shalt rise above defeat and trouble.
4. Thou shalt look upon each day as a new day.
5. Thou shalt always do thy best and leave the rest to God.
6. Thou shalt not waste thy time and energy in useless worry.

7. Thou shalt look only on the bright side of life.
8. Thou shalt not be afraid of tomorrow.
9. Thou shalt have a kind word and a kind deed for everyone.
10. Thou shalt say every morning, "I am a child of God and nothing can hurt me."

Through these positive thoughts, you, too, can realize that the pain of loss is not an enemy to be feared but an experience that makes you more aware of life.

Action

Begin to incorporate these ten principles into your daily lives.

Prayer

Father God, may we learn to take all the negatives of life and turn them into forces for good. Amen.

Reflection

Keep Your Word

A faithful man will abound with blessings.
—PROVERBS 28:20

Scripture Reading: Proverbs 28:16-28

We are repeatedly challenged to understand what it means to be faithful to God. We know we're supposed to be dedicated and committed, but when we see faithfulness wavering in the lives of those around us, it can be difficult to remember what it means to have this virtue. The first thing we must do is look at our actions. When we exhibit the fruit of faithfulness, we show up on time, finish the job, are there when we need to be, and do what we say we are going to do. One of the Barnes' favorite mottoes is: "Just do what you say you are going to do!" Can you imagine what a difference living out this motto would make on the job, with your spouse and children, at church, and in your own life? The results would be amazing!

A successful life is based on trust and faith. Throughout the Old Testament we read of God's faithfulness to the people of Israel. No matter how much the Israelites complained about their situation, God remained true to His chosen people. In the New Testament, Jesus reflected the same loyalty to His heavenly Father. He always sought

God's will. Jesus' faithfulness took Him all the way to the cross so that our sins could be eternally covered.

The Scriptures make it very clear what it means to be faithful. Someday we will stand before God, and He will welcome us into heaven by saying, "Come in! Well done, good and faithful servant!"

Action

Be faithful in your actions today.

Prayer

Father God, You have said that we are to be faithful. We want to be known as faithful people who honor You. Amen.

Reflection

Little by Little

Wise people live in wealth and luxury, but stupid people spend their money as fast as they get it.

—PROVERBS 21:20 GNB

Precious treasure remains in a wise man's dwelling; but a foolish man devours it (RSV).

Scripture Reading: Proverbs 21:16-31

One of the most difficult principles to teach is financial discipline. We are a nation of spenders and consumers, and most of us know little about the importance of saving each month. To be financially independent, we must spend less than we make.

In Thomas Stanley's book *The Millionaire Mind*, he states, "The success of the millionaire is due to his discipline and has little to do with luck or happenstance. It is hard to overemphasize the importance of discipline in accounting for variation is economic success"[11]

There are many wonderful Christian books that can help you establish the discipline to become financially independent, but the bottom line principles include:

- Save little by little.

- Say no to consumable goods that aren't necessary.

- Develop a plan for saving.
- Spend less than you make.
- Use credit cards only if you pay the balance each month.
- Give to the Lord's work on a weekly basis.
- Never gamble or play the lottery.
- If it sounds too good to be true, it probably is.
- Never buy anything from a solicitor over the phone.
- Go into a career you are passionate about.
- Choose a market niche that few people are trying to fill.
- Be willing to take a risk after prayer and wise counsel.
- Believe in yourself.
- Think success, not failure.

Action

Read a book on developing a financial plan. Learn all you can about finance, then set a goal and work toward it.

Prayer

Father God, may we learn Your principles and apply them. Help us to be financially responsible. Amen.

Reflection

Ten Good Friends

Though one may be overpowered by another, two can withstand him. And a threefold cord is not quickly broken.

—ECCLESIASTES 4:12

Scripture Reading: Ecclesiastes 4:8-12

From the very beginning, God knew that it was important for us to have friends. Scripture encourages us to associate with others. God knew that when tough times came we would need people to come alongside and make us stronger than we would normally be.

During Emilie's bout with cancer, we have had the opportunity to witness how a "threefold cord" gives added strength. Just at the time we needed it, we received a card; a phone call; a person delivering flowers, cakes, or a needed casserole; someone willing to run an errand that was needed. Literally thousands of well-wishers have extended themselves to our service. When in need of a bone marrow donor, e-mails were sent by people who wanted to know how they could be a donor candidate. Unbelievable friendships have come at the perfect time.

In today's reading we find King Solomon emphasizing what a blessing friends are:

- "Two are better than one because they have a good reward for their labor" (Ecclesiastes 4:9).

- "Woe to him who is alone when he falls, for he has no one to help him up" (verse 10).

- "If two lie down together, they will keep warm" (verse 11).

- Two can resist one who tries to overpower them (see verse 12).

- A cord of three strands is not easily broken (see verse 12).

Action

Let your friends know how much you appreciate them.

Prayer

Father God, may we begin to develop relationships that have eternal worth. We want three-cord friends! Amen.

Reflection

Always Be Thankful

In everything give thanks; for this is the
will of God in Christ Jesus for you.
—1 THESSALONIANS 5:18

Scripture Reading: Leviticus 23:15-22

Consider what the Lord has done for you and those you love, then give Him thanks with hearts of praise for the blessings from above. But what about all the trials, frustrations, and disappointments in life? Are we to give thanks for those, too?

Yes! We can give thanks whether the day goes as we plan or not. No matter whether we are poor or rich, well or sick, in all of our circumstances we can agree that God is good. Since all things are screened through Him before they ever reach our doorsteps, we can discover how God makes "all things work together for good to those who love [Him]" (Romans 8:28). We are to praise God even when we're not sure how He will work out our situation. Our gratitude is *to* Him and *for* Him.

Action

Give thanks to God about one of your difficult areas. Ask Him what you are to learn through this circumstance.

Prayer

Father God, we are trusting You today to show us Your mighty power in helping us understand what lessons You have for us to learn. Show us how to give thanks in our lives. Amen.

Reflection

~~~~~~~~~~~

*Even though things look cloudy
they'll get better soon.
Just remember that it's true;
it takes rain to make rainbows,
lemons to make lemonade, and
sometimes it takes difficulties to
make us stronger and better people.
The sun will shine again soon...
you'll see.*

—COLLIN MCCARTY

~~~~~~~~~~~

A Prayer of Humble Trust

Lord, I have given up my pride and turned away from my arrogance. I am not concerned with great matters or with subjects too difficult for me. Instead, I am content and at peace. As a child lies quietly in its mother's arms so my heart is quiet within me. Israel, trust in the LORD now and forever!

—PSALM 131 GNB

Scripture Reading: Psalm 131

The psalmist urgently cries out in his despair for the Lord to hear his prayer for forgiveness. His sins overwhelm him, and he feels as though he is drowning. God forgives and the worshiper's gratitude for God's grace leads him to reverent fear and obedience. The poet waits patiently for the Lord's forgiveness. He urges others to wait confidently and expectantly for God.

In order for us to have a quiet heart and peace within, we must confess our sins and be removed from the heavy weight of conviction. We can trust in the Lord's love and compassion now and forevermore.

Action

Go to the Lord and cleanse yourselves of all unrighteousness.

Prayer

Father God, we stand before You right now to ask forgiveness of all our sins. We want to be able to serve You humbly and completely. Amen.

Reflection

~~~~~~~~~~~~~~~~

Prayer can be a form of service in itself. But it also increases our capacity and desire to serve in other ways. When we are coming to the Lord regularly in prayer we are usually growing in compassion, growing in understanding, and growing in our willingness to serve our Heavenly Father.

—GLENN BAXLEY, EMILIE BARNES

~~~~~~~~~~~~~~~~

It Is Well with My Soul

God is our refuge and strength,
a very present help in trouble.
—PSALM 46:1

Scripture Reading: Psalm 46

*H*ow does one recover from the tragedies of life? How does a man make meaning of losing four wonderful daughters in a boating accident while they were traveling to Europe to be with their parents?

Through circumstances unknown, the ship the girls traveled on, the *S.S. Ville du Havre*, was struck by an English vessel and sank in 12 minutes. Two hundred twenty-six drowned, and four of the victims were Tanetta, Maggie, Annie, and Bessie. Their mother was miraculously saved. She sent word by Western Union to her husband, who was assisting D.L. Moody and Ira Sankey in a crusade: "Saved alone. Your wife."

Horatio Spafford immediately took another ship to join his wife in Cardiff, Wales. It is said that when the ship sailed approximately over the spot where his four daughters lost their lives, he was comforted by these words inspired by the Holy Spirit: "When sorrows like sea billows roll—whatever my lot, Thou has taught me to say, it is well with my soul." Three years later, in 1876, Philip P. Bliss took this experience and added music. "It Is Well with My Soul" has inspired millions of people:

> When peace, like a river, attendeth my way,
> When sorrows like sea billows roll;
> Whatever my lot, Thou has taught me to say,
> It is well, it is well, with my soul.

Only by God's grace and His sufficiency could a loving father give meaning to the untimely, tragic death of his daughters.

Life is not always fair, and there aren't always answers to the "whys" of life, but no matter what, we can sing praises to God.

Action

Say with Horatio Spafford, "It is well with my soul," no matter what may be the circumstances that God has allowed.

Prayer

Father God, as Your children we pray that during the difficult trials we can each say, "It is well with my soul." Amen.

Reflection

At the End

I have fought the good fight, I have finished the race,
I have kept the faith.

—2 TIMOTHY 4:7

Scripture Reading: 2 Timothy 4:6-8

As a young couple it was hard for us to look down the pike and see clearly those things that had eternal values. They seemed so very far away. However, as life sped by, we began to contemplate them. Many of the events that concerned us in our younger days seem like fleeting moments now. As we have been fighting this cancer battle, we have been exposed to life and death. We have met people who had to come face-to-face with the brevity of life. In some cases six weeks, six months, or even six years. At those times, we asked, "What's it all about? What will others say about us? Have we done anything of value for God?"

As we shared this reading for today, we both agreed that these three pronouncements would be the bottom line of our life:

- I have fought the good fight.
  - I have finished the race.
    - I have kept the faith.

What is our reward for these three virtues? Paul, in 2 Timothy 4:8, states, "There is laid up for me the crown of righteousness, which the Lord, the righteous Judge, will give to me on that Day, and not to me only but also to all who have loved His appearing."

The Bible only gives a few glimpses of this heavenly abode. Heaven is a place prepared for believers (John 14:1-3) with no sorrow, darkness, or any kind of sin (Revelation 21:1-7). In heaven, we will be like Christ, and we will be able to recognize one another (1 John 3:2; Luke 16:19-31). The most important thing about heaven, however, is the presence of God. We will be forever with Him.

This concept of heaven is not just one for the future, but it is to be lived out in the present. We are to live now in the light of eternity. The values and perspectives of eternity should guide our lives in the present (2 Peter 3:10-18).

Action

Live each day in anticipation of Jesus' return for the church.

Prayer

Father God, as a family we want to live each day so You are glorified. May we be faithful in our walk with You! Amen.

Reflection

Is It Mud or Beauty?

If there is anything praiseworthy—meditate on these things.
—PHILIPPIANS 4:8

Scripture Reading: Philippians 4:2-9

One Sunday morning as we were going to the airport in Maui, Hawaii, it began to rain. The shuttle bus driver said excitedly, "This is a day for celebration." She went on to explain that, in Hawaii, if rain falls on your wedding it will bring good luck. We looked at each other and both agreed that in southern California if it rained on your wedding it would be a disaster. Strange how people look at things differently.

On one rainy day, a woman overheard another person say, "What miserable weather!" The woman looked out of her apartment window to see a big, fat robin using a nearby puddle of water for a bathtub. He was having a wonderful time splashing water everywhere. She thought, "Miserable for whom?"

Another example of such diverse perspective was when a young boy watched an artist paint a picture of a muddy river. The boy told the artist he didn't like the picture because there was too much mud in it. The artist did admit there was mud, but what he saw was the beautiful colors and contrasts of the light against the dark.

Mud or beauty—which do we look for as we travel through life? As Paul taught in today's passage, we are to look for and think about things that are true, honest, just, pure, lovely, of good report, and things with virtue. Look for the best and see the beautiful in everything each day. We have often heard the expression, "What you see is what you get." That's exactly what life is all about. Look beyond the mud and see the beautiful contrasts between the light and the dark. This is the way to get the best out of life.

Action
    Watch for a robin splashing in a pool of water.

Prayer
    Father God, let us look at life with a perspective focused on seeing Your beauty in our surroundings. Amen.

Reflection

"Come, See"

*Come, see a Man who told me all things that
I ever did. Could this be the Christ?*

—John 4:29

Scripture Reading: John 4:27-38

As a young boy I would anxiously wait for the appropriate time on Saturday evening to tune in to one of my favorite radio programs featuring the old-time country western songwriter, singer, and storyteller Stuart Hamblin. I would sit there and visualize every word he said.

Stuart came from a very rough life of drinking, smoking, womanizing, cussing, and denouncing God. He had lived life to the "hilt," but he was a man who had an emptiness to him that made him lonely. His wife, Susie, was a Christian who prayed fervently for her husband's salvation. As the story goes, one evening Stuart got to the end of his rope and proclaimed, "I cannot go on any longer like this." In 1949, at the first Billy Graham Crusade in Los Angeles, Stuart walked that long aisle and accepted Jesus as his personal Savior. From that moment on, he made a 180-degree turn and lived the rest of his life proclaiming who Jesus was and is in his life.

Shortly after Stuart Hamblen's conversion, he wrote a wonderful song that reflected what God had done for him:

> It is no secret what God can do, what He's done
> for others He'll do for you; with arms wide open,
> He'll pardon you—It is no secret what God can do.

As a couple with more than 45 years of married experience walking the walk and talking the talk, we can mightily proclaim, "What Jesus has done for us, He can do for you!"

Action

Be willing to let God change your life.

Prayer

Father God, we are in awe when we hear people share how You have dramatically changed their lives. May our willingness to be obedient open our lives for change. Amen.

Reflection

Be Filled with the Hope of God

*Now may the God of hope fill you with all joy and
peace in believing, that you may abound in hope
by the power of the Holy Spirit.*

—ROMANS 15:13

Scripture Reading: Romans 15:7-13

---

*Y*ou know the old saying, "Where there's life, there's hope"? Well, we would put it a little differently. We'd say, "Without hope, life as we know it is simply impossible." How can we survive without at least a tiny spark of possibility? How can we thrive without a healthy sense of promise? How can we grow unless hope keeps us looking and learning and moving forward? That's what hope really is after all. It's the desire and ability to move ahead. It's a forward-looking attitude and a growing orientation. It's interest and investment in tomorrow. And, oh, how we need that orientation in our lives!

When life crashes and burns—when sickness strikes, a pink slip arrives, a friend lets us down, or we just seem to lose the way, we need hope as a lifeline to pull us through and keep us going toward better times.

We need a hope that is bigger than we are to carry us where our human hope cannot survive. We need a hope that is stronger than death. Even in the darkest, sleepless night, it will hold you.[12] The hope that resides deep inside you is stronger than you think. It's a survival mechanism built into you by the Master Designer. Even when it seems to be ebbing low, if you'll give it a chance, it will bubble back up again.

Action

Spend time with your children, let their youth and enthusiasm rub off on you and freshen your hope.

Prayer

Father God, thank You for the hope You give us by giving us Your Son as our Savior. Amen.

Reflection

Be Careful with Your Scissors

If it is possible, as much as depends on you,
live peaceably with all men.
—ROMANS 12:18

Scripture Reading: Romans 12:9-21

We had an aunt and uncle who always hung the prospect of an inheritance over family members so they would behave a certain way. Often we would leave a family event and laughingly comment that Harry or Mary were no longer in the will because of something that happened during the gathering of the family.

We also knew another woman who was also very good at using scissors to cut out of photographs members of her family and friends who did not measure up. One little slipup and you were "scissored out." If you did not immediately respond positively with great gratitude, you were snipped. Once you were snipped, you were never glued back into the picture.

After many years of doing this type of surgery, the elderly woman passed away. During the funeral preparations, the family hired the police to help with the great traffic jam that was anticipated. Even the local florist, along with the innkeepers, were notified so they knew a large gathering was going to happen. On the day of the funeral, only the husband, a few family members, and very few friends attended the scissors lady's funeral.

When we eliminate imperfect people from our lives, it guarantees loneliness in the end. Live at peace with all people if possible.

Action

Sew back into your pattern of life anyone you may have snipped out.

Prayer

Father God, give us the heart to surround ourselves with friends and family. May we never pick up a pair of scissors and cut someone from our inner circle. Amen.

Reflection

The Secret of Life

Now godliness with contentment is great gain.
—1 TIMOTHY 6:6

Scripture Reading: 1 Timothy 6:1-10

A bishop of the early church who was a remarkable example of contentment was asked his secret for life. He replied, "It consists in nothing more than making a right use of my eyes. In whatever circumstance I am, I first look up to heaven and remember that my principle business here on earth is to get there. I then look down upon the earth, and remember how small a place I shall occupy in it when I die and am buried. I then look abroad in the world and observe what multitudes there are who are in all respects more unhappy then myself. Thus I learn where true happiness is placed, where all our cares must end, and what little reason I have to complain."

One of our family's sayings is: "If you're not content with what you have, you'll never be content with what you want."

We are a country characterized by discontent. Do you find yourself being drawn into this mindset? When we find ourselves looking to the future because we aren't content with today, may God give us a peace of mind that lets us rest where He has placed us. Be content today!

Action

Write a letter to God thanking Him for all your blessings. Name them one by one.

Prayer

Father God, give us rest and help us be content with all You have generously given us. Amen.

Reflection

~~~~~~~~~
Minimize friction and create harmony. You can get friction for nothing, but harmony costs courtesy and self-control.

—AUTHOR UNKNOWN
~~~~~~~~~

Be Alone to Pray

And when He had sent the multitudes away, He went
up on the mountain by Himself to pray.
—MATTHEW 14:23

Scripture Reading: Matthew 14:22-33

Do you feel frustrated when you look at your daily planner? Do you utter words like, "There's no way I can get all I have planned for the day done!"? With all our new technology, we seem to be going faster and faster. No sooner does one microchip come out to speed things up, then we hear cries, "Faster, faster. We need a faster chip."

An old cartoon says it all. Beneath a picture of a frustrated young man was this caption: "God put me on this earth to accomplish a certain number of things. Right now I'm so far behind I will never die."

We complain of packed agendas, endless meetings, long hours, little time with the family, driving our children all over town, church responsibilities, recreation activities, and on and on. "Help, I want off this merry-go-round!" we cry.

If we look at today's passage, we see that Jesus also had endless activities to accomplish. How was He able to do everything and still accomplish His earthly ministry in a sensible way? He made doing His Father's will His top priority. He left the multitudes and prayed.

When you feel closed in and ready to lose your sanity, remember Jesus' example—get away and pray. No one can be a juggler and keep all the balls in motion without taking the time to rest. No one can continue to serve God without being refreshed by Him. In order to make the most of your time, take time to pray.

Action

> Plan a mini-vacation so you can rest and pray together.

Prayer

> *Father God, may our desire to have Your will for our lives be our number-one priority.*

Reflection

The Right Kind of Toughness

A soft answer turns away wrath, but a
harsh word stirs up anger.

—PROVERBS 15:1

Scripture Reading: Proverbs 15:1-7

*A*esop once wrote about gentleness:

Once upon a time when everything could talk, the Wind and the Sun fell into an argument as to which was the stronger. Finally they decided to put the matter to a test; they would see which one could make a certain man, who was walking along the road, throw off his cape. The Wind tried first. He blew and he blew. The harder and colder he blew, the tighter the traveler wrapped the cape about him. The Wind finally gave up and told the Sun to try. The Sun began to smile and as it grew warmer and warmer, the traveler was comfortable once more. But the Sun shone brighter and brighter until the man grew too hot. He became weary, and seating himself on a stone, he quickly threw his

cape to the ground. Gentleness had accomplished
what force could not.

When we look at the gifts of power and strength, isn't
it amazing that gentleness is included? When we see 300-
pound football linemen interviewed on television, it's
surprising to discover that many of these huge men have
a tenderness to their personalities and are dedicated
Christians, loving husbands, and affectionate dads. The
world often equates being gentle with being a coward and
an easy pushover, but we know that is not the case.
Gentleness takes uncommon strength!

A caring person helps an elderly person across the
street. A little girl holds a china cup delicately so it won't
slip and fall to the floor. A mother animal carries her
young tenderly in her mouth. We recognize gentleness
when we see it. As followers of Jesus, our joy is to transfer
and apply this fruit of the Spirit into Christian action. To
attain gentleness, our natural, earthly desires need to
come under the submission of God's will. We will become
all that God wants us to become *when* we reflect a spirit of
gentleness.

Action
Be tough, but be balanced with gentleness.

Prayer
*Father God, please remind us that no matter what the
circumstance we are Your children and that You lift up
those who have gentleness in their spirit. Amen.*

Reflection

He Is My Shepherd

The LORD is my shepherd; I shall not want.
—PSALM 23:1

Scripture Reading: Psalm 23

---

*H*ow easy it is for us to take for granted the phrase "the Lord is my shepherd." Unless we are acquainted with the role of the shepherd in herding sheep, we may not fully understand how valuable the shepherd is. He is the provider, the protector, the security blanket when the wolves of the wild seek their victims for future meals.

David wrote in Psalm 34:10, "The young lions lack and suffer hunger; but those who seek the LORD shall not lack any good thing." That's all we need when we are looking for a good shepherd. C.H. Spurgeon once said, "I have all things and abound; not because I have a good store of money in the bank, not because I have skill and wit with which to win my bread, but because 'The Lord is my shepherd.'"

Once there was a rural pastor in a small eastern community who called the local newspaper to list his Sunday morning message entitled, "The Lord Is My Shepherd." The editor asked the pastor, "Is that all?" The pastor replied back, "That's enough!" On Saturday, when

247

the paper came out, the pastor hurriedly looked in the church section and was shocked when he came to his church's ad. It read: "The Lord Is My Shepherd—That's Enough!" The editor hadn't heard right, but it turned out wonderfully. The truth certainly is: "The Lord is my shepherd—that's enough!" The Lord is sufficient for *all* our needs.

Action

Know that all you need is the Lord. He is sufficient for all situations!

Prayer

Father God, guide us through the soft, green pastures. Let us know all Your goodness. Amen.

Reflection

Use Your Head and Heart

*Fear the LORD, you his saints, for those who fear him
lack nothing....Come, my children, listen to me;
I will teach you the fear of the LORD.*

—PSALM 34:9,11 NIV

Scripture Reading: Psalm 34:9-18 NIV

We live in an age where knowledge doubles and triples by the month and year. With the Internet, young people can research all the data they need or want without ever having human contact. Today's children play games and correspond via e-mail with people they never meet, all with the anonymity that doesn't require truth or, in some cases, positive boundaries.

It's important to teach our children that the human touch is crucial to well-adjusted, contented living. If they rely too much on technology, they will begin to behave as machines and lose the joy of human companionship with others and with God. It is through face-to-face contact with others that we learn to love, to be compassionate, to serve others, and to honor God.

Action

Help your children move beyond the gathering of information and teach them how to touch someone's life with God's love.

Prayer

Father God, give us wisdom to guide our children in today's information age. Help us show them the importance and joys of direct interaction with You and with others. Amen.

Reflection

~~~~~~~

The best things you can give children, next to good habits, are good memories.

—UNKNOWN

~~~~~~~

Two Are Better Than One

A man shall leave his father and mother and be joined to his wife, and they shall become one flesh.

—GENESIS 2:24

Scripture Reading: Matthew 19:1-12

---

*N*ature lets us observe the increased efficiency when there is more than one. A flock of geese increase their flying range by 71 percent when they fly in V-formation. Draft horses dramatically increase the amount of weight they can pull when they are harnessed together. Shouldn't we, as married couples with families, grasp this basic principle of life? Two are better than one!

Yet we try to go it alone. This solitariness will be our destruction; man and woman were not made to be totally independent.

When we were dating, it became obvious that each of us had certain strengths and weaknesses. We also recognized that if we combined our strengths, we would be stronger than if we went our separate ways. To go one step farther, we must rely upon each other's strengths to cover our weaknesses. And that includes spiritual issues. It is easier to resist temptation when we're accountable to someone else.

Action

Discuss areas of weakness that need to be strengthened in order to become a stronger unit.

Prayer

Father God, thank You for reminding us that each of us has strengths that need to be used in our home, family, and marriage. Amen.

Reflection

What Will You Do with Time?

And I will very gladly spend and be spent for your souls.
—2 CORINTHIANS 12:15

Scripture Reading: 2 Corinthians 12:14-21

Oftentimes we hear the adage that we can tell what's important to people by looking at two things in their lives: their checkbooks and their calendars. "When we love something it is of value to us, and when something is of value to us we spend time with it, time enjoying it, and time taking care of it."[13]

Imagine for a moment that your bank suddenly announced this as a new policy: Every morning your account is going to be credited with $86,400. You can carry no balance from day to day. Every evening, your account will be canceled and whatever money you failed to use during the day will be returned to the bank. What would you do? Why, you'd draw out every cent of the money each day and spend it!

Actually, you do have a bank account with a similar policy. It is called *time*. Every morning, you are given the prospect of 86,400 seconds. At the close of that 24-hour period, the moments you failed to withdraw and invest to good purpose are taken out of your ledger. Time carries no balance from day to day, and it allows no overdrafts.

We encourage you to look at time as a very valuable asset. Each moment is very precious; never underestimate its value. When a person, a family, a society lives life on purpose, they become energized in all that they do. Make your days count!

Action

Evaluate how you are spending your 86,400 seconds per day. What needs to be changed?

Prayer

Father God, let us see through the blurred vision of our society and dust off our glasses. Help us see how valuable each second is. Let us spend time in those activities that have eternal value. Amen.

Reflection

People Need People

[Love] bears all things, believes all things, hopes all things, endures all things. Love never fails.

—1 Corinthians 13:7,8

Scripture Reading: 1 Corinthians 13:4-13

Sometimes the smallest gesture of kindness makes all the difference in a person's life. Confusion many times is made clear by just being there for another person.

There's a story about Napoleon when he went to school in Brienne. There he met a young man named Demasis who greatly admired him. After Napoleon quelled the mob in Paris and served at Toulon, his authority was stripped from him and he became penniless. We rarely think of Napoleon as struggling through hard times. However, with thoughts of suicide he proceeded toward a bridge to throw himself into the waters below. On the way, he met his old friend Demasis, who asked him what was so troubling.

Napoleon told him straightforwardly that he was without money, his mother was in need, and he despaired of his situation ever changing. "Oh, if that's all," Demasis said, "take this. It will supply your needs." He put a pouch of gold into Napoleon's hands and walked away. Normally

Napoleon would have never taken such a handout, but that night he did and his hope was renewed.

When Napoleon came to power, he sought far and wide to thank and promote his friend...but he never found him.[14]

Action

Help someone today who needs to be encouraged.

Prayer

Father God, let us be sensitive to people around us who might need a word of encouragement or a gift to help them find their way again. Amen.

Reflection

Living a Happy Life

Whatever you do, do it heartily, as to the Lord.
—COLOSSIANS 3:23

Scripture Reading: Colossians 3:1-4,16-24

Each of us has a special calling to be used as a worker of God. Some people will be plowers, some planters, some reapers. Many times these jobs are outside our everyday occupations. Take time to look at your life together and figure out how your service to God is going. We've found that couples who take time to write out their "mission goals" and look to the future are excited and energized.

Our suggestion for living a happy life is to live life with purpose. Give yourself away to a cause. Andrew Murray said, "I have learned to place myself before God every day as a vessel to be filled with His Holy Spirit. He has given me the blessed assurance that He, as the everlasting God, has guaranteed His own work in me."

Do what you like to do before the Lord, and do it with all the energy and creativity you have, regardless of the social ranking or prestige of the calling.

Action

Write down three desires you have for your life together. How are you going to get there?

Prayer

Father God, give us the vision and desire to do Your work. Reveal to us what we must do to accomplish Your goals for us. Amen.

Reflection

~~~~~~~~
*The key to maintaining
a disciplined life is a
lifetime of perseverance.*
—RHONDA KELLEY
~~~~~~~~

Gaining Self-Control

But also for this very reason, giving all diligence, add to your faith virtue, to virtue knowledge, to knowledge self-control, to self-control perseverance, to perseverance godliness, to godliness brotherly kindness, and to brotherly kindness love.

—2 Peter 1:5-7

Scripture Reading: 2 Peter 1:1-11

An important step to gaining self-control is writing down easy-to-follow steps to reach our goals. If we write these out in clear terms and give ourselves a date for completion, we will be well on our way to experiencing a fulfilling Christian walk. And the best news is that we don't have to do it all on our own! The power of the Holy Spirit will enable us to master any wavering in our commitment. Seek out His leading, and you will be ushered into a satisfying, new life of self-control.

In Romans 7:15-25, the apostle Paul deals with this classic problem when he struggles to exercise self-control in his life. In verses 18,19, he says: "I have the desire to do what is good, but I cannot carry it out. For what I do is not the good I want to do; no, the evil I do not want to do—this I keep on doing" (NIV). Like Paul, we must often cultivate the fruit of self-control so it will grow in our lives and help us do what is right. To do this, we need to recognize our weaknesses and vulnerabilities and desire self-control in our hearts.

Action

Minimize friction and create harmony today.

Prayer

Father God, we thank You for being a patient God, one who walks beside us as we take baby steps in our growth toward self-control. Amen.

Reflection

~~~~~~~

The [person] who wants to make a difference must seek inner strength instead of self-sufficiency.

—JOYCE B. GAGE

~~~~~~~

Build a Hedge

No evil shall befall you.
—PSALM 91:10

Scripture Reading: Psalm 91:9-16

With so many couples working outside of the home, it is important that we pray "hedges" around our spouses so that no evil shall befall them. And, as our society continues to devalue our family structure, we need to place an even greater emphasis on prayers of protection. Husbands and wives are bombarded by Satan. He would love to destroy the love that we have for each other, our focus on the Lord, our prayer lives, our commitment to church, our consistency in Bible reading, and our relationships with our children.

Make it a habit to continually be in prayer for your mate as you go through the day. Share with each other your schedules for the day so you know when extra prayer support is needed. When traveling away from home, be sure to take some reminders from home—a family picture, a present that was given before departing, artwork from the children, a Bible—anything to help you focus on what's really important to you.

Action

How comforting it is to know that our mates pray for us. Make it a habit to pray for your mate each day.

Prayer

Father God, we pray that You will protect us from all evil. Build a protective hedge around our lives. Amen.

Reflection

Love Is More Than One Word

*"You shall love the LORD your God with all your heart,
with all your soul, with all your strength, and with
all your mind," and "your neighbor as yourself."*

—LUKE 10:27

Scripture Reading: Deuteronomy 6:4-9

Our passage for today talks about three basic loves: love of God, love of neighbor, and love of self. What a difference Christians would make in this world if we were able to truly love this way! In Ephesians 5:18-21, it tells us if we are loving ourselves we will speak and sing words of joy. Our lives will be characterized by delight, praise, and enthusiasm. If we are loving God, we will give thanks for all things in the name of our Lord Jesus Christ.

If we acknowledge that God created us, recognize that the Holy Spirit lives in us, and realize that Jesus gave His life for us, we'll know we have value as individuals and as God's children.

If we love others, we will be able to be subject to one another in the fear of Christ. We will be less selfish and, therefore, able to willingly set aside some of our perceived needs in our relationships.

The commands to love God with all our hearts, all our souls, all our strength, and all our minds, and to love others and ourselves are a call to put first things first. It's a daily challenge to do so.

Action

Discuss with your mate how you can live out your love for God, others, and yourself.

Prayer

Father God, help us to start our day by asking: "What can we do to love You with all our hearts, souls, minds, and strength?" Help us put our love into practice. Amen.

Reflection

Listen to Words of Knowledge

*Apply your heart to instruction, and
your ears to words of knowledge.*
—PROVERBS 23:12

Scripture Reading: Proverbs 23:12-20

When a child is allowed to roam without any boundaries, tragedy usually follows. One of the saddest results is when a child loses his or her life because the parents never established the discipline of authority and respect.

A family had taken shelter in the basement as a severe storm passed over their town. The radio warned that a tornado had been spotted. When the storm had passed by, the father opened the front door to look at the damage. A downed power line was whipping dangerously on the street in front of their house. Before the father realized what was happening, his five-year-old daughter ran right by him, headed for that sparkling wire in the street.

"Laurie, stop!" he yelled. Laurie just kept going.

"Laurie, stop!" Laurie ran right for the enticing cable.

"Stop now, Laurie!"

Little Laurie reached down to pick up the wicked power line and was instantly killed."[15]

What a heart-breaking tragedy! But the real tragedy is that this happened because a little girl had never been taught that when her father said no, he really meant it. It cost him the life of his daughter.

One of the roles we have as a parent is to be teachers. We should continually be on the lookout for situations that afford us the opportunity to teach our children. If we do, our children will be able to hear and heed our commands knowing we have knowledge and their best interest on our side. How we train our little ones today is more than likely how the next three generations will live.

It is up to us, as parents, to stand in the gap and hang tough. This is not an easy battle (and it is truly a battle), for the evil one would like us to give in to the path of least resistance. We must be willing to travel the road less traveled even if it entails conflict and discipline.

Action

Instruct your children so they will hear your words of knowledge.

Prayer

Father God, give us humble hearts and the determination to teach our children godly principles. When they hear instruction, help them respond in a positive way. Amen.

Reflection

Noah's Favor

Noah found grace in the eyes of the LORD.
—GENESIS 6:8

Scripture Reading: Genesis 6:8-22

Noah lived in a sin-filled world much like ours today. Human beings haven't changed much over the years; we just call sin by different names now. Even though there was great wickedness around Noah, he lived a life that was pleasing to God. Noah didn't find favor because of his individual goodness. He stood out because of his faith.

Although Noah was upright and blameless before God, he wasn't perfect. Genuine faith does not always mean perfect faith. Even with his human failings, Noah walked a righteous path. The events of his life could have blocked his fellowship with God, but his heart qualified him to find favor with God.

You and I are judged by the same standard Noah was. Are we faithful and obedient to God? Whose favor are we looking for—the honor of people or the honor of God? The world puts its favors in beautiful packages with glitzy bows. Be careful not to be sucked in by all the spotlights and glitter.

Action

Find another couple you trust to hold you accountable for your Christian walk.

Prayer

Father God, sometimes it seems like we are the only ones standing up for righteousness. Please encourage us to hang in and fight the battle. Help us find another couple we can share with. Amen.

Reflection

~~~~~~~~~~

Even the most tragic happenings will be turned into good for those who love the Lord and are His children. Our spiritual rearing is moved along by the difficulties we face and the mountains we climb.

—DOROTHY KELLEY PATTERSON

~~~~~~~~~~

The Greatest Prayer Ever Prayed

Our Father in heaven, hallowed be Your name.
Your kingdom come. Your will be done
on earth as it is in heaven.
Give us this day our daily bread.
And forgive us our debts, as we forgive our debtors.
And do not lead us into temptation, but deliver us
from the evil one. For Yours is the kingdom and
the power and the glory forever. Amen.

—MATTHEW 6:9-13

Scripture Reading: Matthew 6:1-13

would like to pray, but I don't know how!" Try "The Lord's Prayer." This great prayer was uttered by Jesus to give His followers a model on how to pray. In Jesus' day, the Jews did not address God directly as Father, but they used "Father" to describe God's relationship to Israel or to refer to Him as Creator. "Our Father," or Abba, was a new, more personal title used by Jesus. It carries the more intimate sense of "Daddy," and He invited all who belong to Him to do the same (Galatians 4:6).

The beauty and power of The Lord's Prayer is better understood when we look at the individual phrases:

- Our Father in heaven—We must recognize who He is—the very person of God.

- Hallowed be Your name—Worship God because of who He is.

- Your kingdom come. Your will be done—In time God's kingdom will come. We are to do God's will (we find His will by studying the Bible).

- Give us this day our daily bread—Ask God to meet our needs so we can perform His work.

- And forgive us our debts, as we forgive our debtors—Ask God for pardon and forgiveness in our daily failures.

- And do not lead us into temptation, but deliver us from the evil one—Ask God for protection and that we might flee from all evil.

- For Yours is the kingdom and the power and the glory forever—Praise God for who He is. He never changes; He always has been and He always will be.

- Amen—May all this be done in Your Name.

Action
Memorize this model prayer.

Prayer
Father God, this prayer is so soothing and comforting to the soul. It gives us such great support and encouragement in time of need. Thank You. Amen.

Reflection

Welcome Testing and Trials

*My Redeemer lives...[and] this I know, that
in my flesh I shall see God.*

—Job 19:25,26

Scripture Reading: Job 19:13-27

O That Will Be Glory

*When all my labors and trials are o'er,
And I am safe on that beautiful shore,
Just to be near the dear Lord I adore
Will through the ages be glory for me.*

—Charles Gabriel

O ur three-year fight with cancer has been the height of our Christian experience. There are several "dreads" in life, and one of them is to have your doctor tell you that you have cancer with a large tumor in your stomach. When the doctor told us about Emilie's condition, our hearts sank, tears welled, we envisioned death, and our dreams came crashing down. And we've seen our reactions mirrored in the lives of others who have faced this terrible disease. Our faith came to its greatest test. No more dozing as we read Scripture, no more nodding off as we uttered those prayers half-heartedly, no more singing hymns without contemplating their meaning. We were faced with one of the biggest decisions of our life together. Did all that we professed have

271

the same trust we had previously claimed? Did we still have hope? Would bitterness take control? Were we going to trust all of God's promises or were they just poetic words in literature?

Just as Job searched for meaning to all he was going through, we, too, tried to find truer meaning to life. Deep within us our trust in the Lord and all of His promises withstood the trials we were enduring. With shouts of joy and praise, we knew that we were living out God's plan for our lives. We continue to trust Him every step of the way.

Action

Don't wait for one of the dreads of life to fall upon you before you truly trust your faith. Give God His desired praise today!

Prayer

Father God, don't let us get complacent about our faith. Continue to keep us alert when we experience the events You have planned for our lives. Amen.

Reflection

Someone's Looking

Be an example to the believers...in love,
in spirit, in faith, in purity.
—1 TIMOTHY 4:12

Scripture Reading: Nehemiah 5:1-16

Many interviews with wealthy and/or popular personalities include the question: "Are you a role model?" The people usually hesitantly reply, "I don't want to be a role model. Don't look to me as an example." The idea that they are role models scares them. All of us are role models whether we like it or not.

As parents and adults, we have precious young eyes of children looking up at us. They want to be just like us. They walk, they talk, they react to people just like we do. If we yell, they yell; if we compliment, they will compliment; if we use edifying language, so will they.

Children, especially your own, will grasp more by watching you than by hearing your words. Lead them by your example.

Action

Evaluate how you're leading. Make changes where necessary.

Prayer

> Father God, help us guard our actions so that those look-
> ing to us will see Christ. We want to build up people
> and lead them to You. Amen.

Reflection

You're teaching a lesson each day that you live:
Your actions are blazing a trail
That others will follow for good or for ill;
You'll help them or cause them to fail.
—BOSCH

Bearing Good Children

*A good tree cannot bear bad fruit, nor can a bad
tree bear good fruit.*

—MATTHEW 7:18

Scripture Reading: Matthew 7:15-20

As parents we are continually challenged by raising good children—not chemists, not computer whizzes, not star athletes—just good children. Many of us spend so much of our time raising well-behaved, socially adjusted children that we don't concentrate much on teaching moral and ethical values.

We all want our children to do better than we have done, but we often forget that children will rarely display a higher standard of ambition, virtue, character, or godliness than that which we reflect. As parents, we also can't expect someone else to do a better job with our children than we have done. We are the true educators of our children; all others are part of the supporting cast. Do not be willing to turn this important role over to others. We are accountable to God to raise our children according to sound biblical principles.

Action

List five godly characteristics you would like to develop in your children. How can you do it?

Prayer

Father God, give us the desire to be accountable to You for our children. Amen.

Reflection

〜〜〜〜〜〜〜

The most important filter your child can have in any decision-making process is the Word of God.

—SUSAN ALEXANDER YATES

〜〜〜〜〜〜〜

Pursue Peace

Peace I leave with you, My peace I give to you.
—JOHN 14:27

Scripture Reading: John 14:25-31

Peace symbols adorn buses, backpacks, and bumper stickers, and peace itself is pleaded for everywhere and in every language. Lasting peace is certainly what we need. Defined by the fruit of the Spirit, this state is a Christian virtue of assured quietness of the soul. It is the opposite of our earthly struggles, and it is best described as a "wellness between oneself and God."

The peace that God gives is built on the awareness that we all have purpose and cause for existing. As we mature in our spiritual nature and learn what this life is all about, we discover that only our heavenly Father can give us a lasting calmness within. Once we realize this, we no longer toss and turn, trying to find answers to our daily struggles. We have reconciled with God through Jesus, His Son, that life has meaning and we are created in God's image. We know the Alpha and the Omega. We finally know who we are. We have inner tranquility of mind, soul, and spirit. There is a calmness to our presence that is recognizable. Kenneth W. Osbeck states, "Experience the perfect peace of God in your life by realizing anew that it is only obtained through the presence of Christ in our lives—He is our peace."

Our lives reflect God's love and joy, and those around us will be lifted up by our outward expression of this fruit of the Spirit.

Action

Live in peace with one another.

Prayer

Father God, may we continue to be willing and patient to develop our lives toward the precious virtue of peace. Amen.

Reflection

Learn from Our Animals

*In his hand is the life of every creature and
the breath of all mankind.*

—JOB 12:10 NIV

Scripture Reading: Job 12:1-10

All of God's creatures have been given keen
instincts to help them survive under adverse
circumstances. Since we live in southern
California, we are accustomed to having earthquakes. We
have observed over the years that nature gives advance
warnings of earthquakes and other disasters, and many
animals are capable of sensing the impending danger. For
example, our dogs will become restless and let out loud
barks before the seismic upheaval begins. Our cat jumps
on the bed seeking a safe hiding place. Some people have
even recalled that fish are very sensitive and increase their
speed of swimming. Birds will fly out of threatened areas
before an earthquake, and ants will pick up their egg sacs
and move them to a safe spot. Even bears and tigers will
sleep in the open to avoid being trapped in their dens by
falling rocks.

God, the Creator of the universe, has equipped His creatures to help them survive. By watching our animals and pets, we can be warned of the dangers about to occur.

Action

Become students of your animals. It may save your lives.

Prayer

Father God, make us more sensitive to the animals around us. After all, You created them, too. Amen.

Reflection

Love Your Enemies

Love your enemies, bless those who curse you,
do good to those who hate you.
—MATTHEW 5:44

Scripture Reading: Matthew 5:43-48

---

braham Lincoln once said, "The best way to destroy an enemy is to make him your friend." With the polarization of values in America and the increased pressure of everyday living, we find more and more evidence of rage. There are ample evidences that it is becoming easier and easier to have enemies. Even among Christians there are disagreements that fester into anger and harsh feelings. Conflicts can range from simple disagreements within our own family to a serious problem with a fellow worker in the office.

What can we do to ease the tension? Jesus gives us a good example of how to treat those who disagree with us. A good starting place is for us to pray for those who despitefully use us (Matthew 5:44). If we spend time talking to our heavenly Father about those who treat us wrongfully, we'll have a much easier time loving and blessing them. It's very difficult to mistreat someone we have just prayed for.

Action

Ask God to bless those people who fervently disagree with you.

Prayer

Father God, give us the humility to earnestly pray for those who harbor ill against us. Help us to love them as You would. Amen.

Reflection

~~~~~~~

To forgive is to set a prisoner free and discover the prisoner was you.

—UNKNOWN

~~~~~~~

Fertilizer Sure Helps

I planted, Apollos watered, but God gave the increase.
—1 CORINTHIANS 3:6

Scripture Reading: 1 Corinthians 3:1-9

A Sunday school teacher wanted to impress her young pupils with the miracle of life in nature. She pointed to a large plant in the room and asked, "Who made those beautiful flowers grow?" An answer came back quickly from one of the boys in her class. "God did!" She was very pleased with the response, but before she had a chance to comment, another student replied, "But fertilizer sure helps!" This young person made us aware that even though the Lord created this world and the life on and within it, He put us in the garden to tend and cultivate it.

In the last few years we have prayed fervently to God for a healing of the cancer that plagued Emilie. We believe God will, but at the same time we are so thankful to Dr. Barth, our oncologist, who is adding fertilizer along the way. We know that God sometimes uses a team approach, and He is guiding our doctors to give us the increase. God alone is the one who makes things grow, but we know He works through people, including you, to help others.

Action

God is faithful in doing His part. Are you faithful in doing yours? Go out today and spread some fertilizer.

Prayer

Father God, use us today to be faithful in doing our part to help You do Your part. Amen.

Reflection

~~~~~~~~~~

An iron is fashioned by fire and on an anvil, so in the fire of suffering and under the weight of trials, our souls receive the form which our Lord desires them to have.

—St. Madeline Sophie Barat

~~~~~~~~~~

Having a Healthy Family

And Adam said: "This is now bone of my bones and flesh of my flesh; she shall be called Woman, because she was taken out of Man."

—GENESIS 2:23

Scripture Reading: Genesis 2:20-25

The Bible is very clear in its teaching that woman was created for man as his helper. And since "it is not good that man should be alone," both the man and the woman were designed for each other. That was God's plan. Marriage causes a man to leave his mother and father and be united to his wife, becoming one flesh with her. Scripture continues, "The man and his wife were both naked, and they felt no shame" (Genesis 2:25 NIV). Nakedness isn't always physical—it also includes emotional, spiritual, and psychological exposure. One of our biggest challenges in life is to stand before each other, not being ashamed because we have followed God's plan for our family.

When all else fails, follow God's instruction book—the Bible. Become one spiritually, emotionally, and physically.

You'll be amazed at how strong your marriage can become.

Action

Be more open with your spouse. Risk being naked before each other. Be transparent.

Prayer

Father God, help us become more aware of what each of us can do to be more understanding of our differences. Amen.

Reflection

I've Learned from Yesterday

Barnabas was determined to take with them John called Mark. But Paul insisted that they should not take with them the one who had departed from them.

—ACTS 15:37,38

[Paul said,] Get Mark and bring him with you, for he is useful to me for ministry.

—2 TIMOTHY 4:11

Scripture Reading: Acts 15:36-41

When I've failed, I need You, Lord,
To teach this lesson clear:
If we would learn and try again,
Success may soon be near.

—BRANON

Have you ever wished that you could go back in time and undo a failure? We have. And we know of couples who wish that they could undo an act, a word, a facial expression, or an event in their early marriage. However impossible this is, we can learn from our mistakes.

In today's reading, we find such an episode where John Mark accompanied Paul and Barnabas when they started out in their first missionary journey, but he soon deserted them (see Acts 13:13). While he was at home he must have regretted what he had done because his uncle, Barnabas, wanted to include him on their next mission trip. Paul said no, then teamed with Silas instead. Mark was probably devastated by this, but he did rise above his first mistake and became a great Christian leader of his day. Eventually, he also won Paul's respect.

Wishing you could do something over is energy wasted. Instead, start where you left off and do all you can to remedy the situation and move forward.

Action

Get ahead of that first defeat. Evaluate the situation, then get on with your life.

Prayer

Father God, let us learn from our failures. Help us to move forward in what You have given us to do. Amen.

Reflection

Too Busy

Six days you shall labor and do all your work,
but the seventh day is the Sabbath of the LORD your God.
In it you shall do no work.
—EXODUS 20:9,10

Scripture Reading: Exodus 20:8-11

The more technology we have, the faster we go. Everyone wants it now—not in five minutes—right now. The faster we go, the farther behind we get! The merry-go-round keeps spinning faster and faster, and we don't know how to get off.

> Suppose you come upon a man in the woods feverishly sawing down a tree.
>
> "You look exhausted!" you exclaim. "How long have you been at it?"
>
> "Over five hours," he replies, "and I'm beat. This is hard."
>
> "Maybe you could take a break for a few minutes and sharpen that saw. Then the work would go faster."
>
> "No time," the man says emphatically. "I'm too busy sawing."[16]

Like all of His commands, God's order to keep the Sabbath, to take time for rest, is for your own good. Don't be fearful of putting down the saw to sharpen it. God will redeem your time.

Action

Stop what you are doing and take time to renew yourselves by sharpening your saw.

Prayer

Father God, living a balanced life seems like an unreachable goal. Help us. Teach us moderation, and show us balance. Amen.

Reflection

Being Too Organized

I know your works, that you have a name that you are alive, but you are dead.

—REVELATION 3:1

Scripture Reading: Revelation 3:1-6

There was a foreign soldier who was wounded and ordered to go to the military hospital for treatment. When he arrived at the large structure he saw two doors—one labeled "For the slightly wounded" and the other "For the seriously wounded."

He entered through the first door and found himself going down a long hall. At the end of it were two more doors, one marked "For officers" and the other, "For enlisted personnel." He entered through the second door and found himself going down another long hall. At the end of it were two more doors, one marked "For party members" and the other "For nonparty members." He took the second door, and when he opened it he found himself out on the street.

Wow! What organization—but the hospital was dead. That's the way it can be with us if we aren't careful. Many of us are highly organized. We are busy and always on the go. Being organized is very important but our priority is to allow the Holy Spirit to work through us freely so others will see Christ in us.

Action

Evaluate whether your compulsion to being organized hinders the Holy Spirit from working in your lives? Do any changes need to be made?

Prayer

Father God, help us be flexible enough in our organization that You are free to work effectively in our lives. Amen.

Reflection

Attitude Check

Let this mind be in you which was also in Christ Jesus.
—PHILIPPIANS 2:5

Scripture Reading: Philippians 2:1-8

When our grandson, Chad, was 15 years old, we gave him the customary card with the number of years represented by brand-new $1 bills. For his gift, we gave him a drinking mug that had a capital A on one side and ATTITUDE printed on the other side. This was a daily reminder to check his attitude, an area of life that can give us all trouble. Attitude is so important in life; without a good one we will never succeed. With a good outlook, we can conquer almost any hurdle.

Genuine humility is a great start. Having the mind and heart and attitude of Christ is the heart of positive attitude. As we study the life of Christ, we see that His willingness to serve had its roots in His confidence that God loved Him. That He was valuable to His Father gave Jesus the strength and security He needed. This knowledge enabled Him to serve people and, ultimately, die for us sinful human beings. Knowing our value to God is the first step toward true humility.

Action

Do an attitude check today. Ask your spouse how you're doing.

Prayer

Father God, we want our attitudes to be pleasing to You. Direct us along Your path. Amen.

Reflection

Don't Stop Listening

A wise man will hear and increase learning, and a man of understanding will attain wise counsel.

—PROVERBS 1:5

Scripture Reading: Proverbs 16:16-23

It's funny how we meet some young people who assert they know it all and nothing can be taught them. On the other hand, we meet elderly people who can't get enough of learning. One such friend of ours, Mary, is 91 years old. She cleans, shops, drives, cooks, gardens (she even climbs a ladder to prune her fruit trees). In conversation with her it's obvious she wants to learn. She continually asks why and how, and is always stretching her mind to new horizons, never satisfied that she already knows all that life has to offer.

The Hebrew word for "learning" in today's verse means "a taking in." If we desire to grow in our knowledge of God and learn to please Him, we need to be willing to discard old ideas and take in new ones that more adequately explain the Scriptures. People who are seekers welcome new ideas. Are you willing to listen, to be tested, to learn?

Action

Learn one new truth today.

Prayer

Father God, help us to listen to new ideas. Prevent our pride from stopping us as we evaluate them. Amen.

Reflection

~~~~~~~~~~~~~~~~

Be at Peace

Be at peace. Do not look forward in fear to the changes of life; rather look to them with full hope as they arise.

God, whose very own you are, will deliver you from out of them. He has kept you hitherto, and He will lead you safely through all things; and when you cannot stand it, God will bury you in His arms.

Do not fear what may happen tomorrow; the same everlasting Father who cares for you today will take care of you then and every day.

He will either shield you from suffering or will give you unfailing strength to bear it.

Be at peace and put aside all anxious thoughts and imaginations.

—St. Francis

~~~~~~~~~~~~~~~~

Notes

Twenty-Six Guards
   1. Source unknown, adapted.

A Ship in the Night
   2. Dennis and Barbara Rainey, *Building Your Mate's Self-Esteem* (San Bernardino, CA: Here's Life Publishers, 1986), pp. 56-57, adapted.

Amazing Grace
   3. Kenneth W. Osbeck, *Twenty-Five Most Treasured Gospel Hymn Stories* (Grand Rapids, MI: Kregel Publications, 1999), p. 13.

Which One Is Adopted?
   4. *God's Little Devotional Book for Dads* (Tulsa, OK: Honors Books, Inc., 1995), p. 59.

Only Eighteen Inches
   5. Adapted from Emilie Barnes, *Cup of Hope* (Eugene, OR: Harvest House Publishers, 2000), pp. 27-29.

Living Through a Terrible Day
   6. Emilie Barnes, *Cup of Hope* (Eugene, OR: Harvest House Publishers, 2000), pp. 71-73.

A Child of the King
   7. Kenneth W. Osbeck, comp. *Amazing Grace: 366 Hymn Stories for Personal Devotions* (Grand Rapids, MI: Kregel Publications, 1990), p. 221. Used by permission.

Be Doers of the Word
   8. Edgar Guest, quoted in the *Seattle Times*, Religion Section, Saturday, May 20, 2000, p. D8.

What Do You See?
   9. *Seattle Times*, Religion Section, Saturday, May 20, 2000, p. D8.

What Makes a Church Alive?

    10.   From an article by Reverend Dale Turner, quoted in the *Seattle Times* Religion Section, Saturday, May 20, 2000, p. D8.

Little by Little

    11.   Stanley, *Millionaire Mind*, pp. 83-84.

Be Filled with the Hope of God

    12.   Adapted from Emilie Barnes, *A Cup of Hope* (Eugene, OR: Harvest House Publishing, 2000), pp. 5-8.

What Will You Do with Time?

    13.   *God's Little Devotional Book for Dads* (Tulsa, OK: Honor Books, Inc., 1995), p. 72.

People Need People

    14.   Whether this story is true or not, the principle remains.

Listen to Words of Knowledge

    15.   Steve Farrar, *Standing Tall* (Sisters, OR: Multnomah Books, 1994), pp. 51-52.

Too Busy

    16.   Stephen Covey, 1990.

Books by Emilie and Bob

~~~~~

15-Minute Devotions for Couples
The 15-Minute Meal Planner
The 15-Minute Money Manager
The 15-Minute Organizer
15 Minutes Alone with God
15 Minutes Alone with God for Men
15 Minutes of Peace with God
Beautiful Home on a Budget
Cooking Up Fun in the Kitchen
A Cup of God's Love
A Cup of Hope
Decorating Dreams on a Budget
Emilie's Creative Home Organizer
Fill My Cup, Lord
Grateful Hearts Give Thanks
Help Me Trust You, Lord
If Teacups Could Talk
An Invitation to Tea
Let's Have a Tea Party!
A Little Book of Manners
A Little Book of Manners for Boys
Making My Room Special
Minute Meditations for Men
Minute Meditations for Women
My Best Friends and Me
My Cup Overflows
What Makes a Man Feel Loved

~~~~~